Francis Gerry Fairfield

Ten Years with Spiritual Mediums

An Inquiry Concerning the Spiritual

Francis Gerry Fairfield

Ten Years with Spiritual Mediums
An Inquiry Concerning the Spiritual

ISBN/EAN: 9783337340797

Printed in Europe, USA, Canada, Australia, Japan

Cover: Foto ©Lupo / pixelio.de

More available books at **www.hansebooks.com**

TEN YEARS

WITH

SPIRITUAL MEDIUMS:

AN INQUIRY CONCERNING
THE ETIOLOGY OF CERTAIN PHENOMENA
CALLED SPIRITUAL.

BY
FRANCIS GERRY FAIRFIELD.

ENTERED, according to Act of Congress, in the year 1874,
BY D. APPLETON & COMPANY,
In the Office of the Librarian of Congress, at Washington.

PREFATORY NOTE.

IN the following pages the author submits the results of ten years of observation and experiment, conducted in the intervals of other work, concerning the nature of certain phenomena confidently relied upon by spiritualists as demonstrative of the agency of departed spirits, and by Prof. Crookes as proving the existence of a force termed *psychic*. In these investigations it has been a fixed principle with me to accept only verified testimony as to the facts, preferring that of medical observers. The reader is to understand, therefore, that the facts stated herein invariably rest either upon observation and experiment personally conducted, or upon the veracity of accredited scientific witnesses; and, in all cases where any room for doubt existed, I have been at the pains to investigate personally, and to accept or reject upon test of actual observation. I am prepared to stand sponsor, therefore, for the various observations, medical and physiological, which I have had occasion to detail in putting my memoranda in form.

Mainly, however, I have relied upon observations personally verified, and experiments personally instituted, on the ground that compilation can never be thoroughly intelligent. Until a man has actually dissected a brain, he knows very little about one, however lucid may be the explanations in the text-books, however accurate the illustrations. At the same time, while carefully verifying, it has not been my intention to produce an elaborate treatise, but simply to make clear to the reader's mind, from physiological induction and by experiment, that the phenomena called spiritual are morbid nervous phenomena, to indicate their etiology, and to trace out their various philosophical relations.

F. G. F.

CONTENTS.

		PAGE
I.	Preliminary Observations	7
II.	Method of Investigation and Summary of Conclusions	18
III.	Cases of Nervo-Psychic Phenomena	34
IV.	Physiology of the Nervo-Psychic Series	92
V.	Nerve-Atmosphere and its Agency in Nervo-Molecular Physics	114
VI.	Memoranda of Nervo-Dynamic Phenomena	134
VII.	Physiology of the Volition and Intelligence involved in the Foregoing Series	159
VIII.	A Glance at the Higher Relations of the Subject	179

TEN YEARS

WITH

SPIRITUAL MEDIUMS.

I.

PRELIMINARY OBSERVATIONS.

ON the night of October 14th, after the red scrimmage at Jena, which was to Prussia in 1806 what Sadowa was to Austria in 1866, a notable coincidence befell.

While Napoleon was dictating orders for the next day in that dull university town, having that memorable afternoon shattered a state, two lights glimmered from the windows of two adjacent houses. The one was the study-lamp of Hegel (to whom the stars were but a brilliant leprosy on the face of the heavens), who was at that moment engaged in demonstrating that history, a notable turning-point of which had that day been settled, is but a manifestation of the *anima mundi*—Latin for world-soul.

The other was that of a journeyman cobbler, since differenced from other cobblers as the cobbler of Jena, who (in detestable doggerel that, in company with volumes of other doggerel not less detestable, has descended to posterity) was busy with a rhyming criticism on General von Blunderhead and his staff:

> "To force the passes of the Saale
>   They thought no enemy would try,
> But then the passes of the Saale
>   They should with cannon fortify;
> Whoever overlookèd this
> Didn't understand his business."

A remarkable juxtaposition this!—belonging to the gossip of history, but no less remarkable for that. The maker, the philosopher, and the satirist of history—three men, of whom the cobbler may have been the greatest, for aught the world knows—grouped together of a night in the same dingy little town, plying their respective but kindred vocations!

Now, those who think with Hegel, that the world has a soul, will not hesitate to find in this picturesque coincidence a dash of the grim humor that occasionally appears in historical events, and to hold the *anima mundi* responsible for it; while those who have outlived their dream of an *anima mundi*, will perforce refer the tableau to the category of fortuitous accidents: for, for the purposes of the present investigation, mankind naturally fall into two classes, namely, those who suppose the world has a soul, and those who through troublous cogitation have disabused themselves of that beautiful but experimentally undemonstrated fancy.

But, were beauty reason for believing — and a man, like a woman, often feels his way to truth faster than he can reason his way thither—Hegel's theory of a world-soul, at once the poet and artist of Nature, would long since have been accepted as fact, in lieu of haunting our lives as a mystic dream, too weird to be admitted into the list of realities, but too beautiful to be rejected.

According to this theory, which, under various forms, thoroughly leavens modern literature, man is a denizen of two worlds—the one subsensible, and pervaded and moved by psychic forces, the other sensible, and subject to the operation of physical forces; and so far has scientific investigation tended to sustain this hypothesis, fanciful as it appears, that it is now conceded by many scientific men that two distinct forces, the one physical, the other psychical, enter into all our experiences and constitute their basis.

Whether the natures of these forces are modifications of the same ultimate reality, or whether they constitute parallel series of realities—these, on the other hand, are questions upon which scientific men are far from coincident. Prof. Huxley and Herbert Spencer appear to accept the first position; and Prof. Tyndall indicates his coincidence in his second lecture on light, when he maintains that a man cannot consider, far less answer the question of what light is, without transporting himself to a world that underlies the sensible one, and out of which, in accordance with rigid law, all optical phenomena spring. The realization of this subsensible world is a task the learned lecturer delegates to the imagination as its function in scientific inquiry. On the contrary, Sir David Brewster dissents from the position of these eminent gentlemen, and nods his scientific yes to the theory of a parallel series of realities.

From this balancing of man upon a pivot between two worlds has arisen a material hypothesis of the soul, the exponents of which assume that our physical organizations are pervaded with an attenuated and subsensible substance, in which the psychical force resides, and which withdraws from the sensible organism at death, a psychical and subsensible entity, individual still, but a denizen of the subsensible world that, according to Prof. Tyndall, underlies the sensible one. The general aspects of this theory have been so well developed by Sergeant Cox as to render original definition unnecessary. His propositions are:

That the material universe is encompassed with spirit pervading it everywhere, not individuated but in aggregation, as the atmosphere envelops the earth.

That this spirit-substance penetrates all matter and moulds it to all shapes.

That in organic beings it becomes a distinct individuality and operates through the vital force that moves all organic structures.

That this spirit possesses the germ, grows with it to maturity, and is released from it at the cessation of organic life.

That exactly as the material atoms pass from mineral to vegetable, and from vegetable to animal structure, so spirit advances from being a mere protoplasm of spirit, by the same process of expansion and progression, to have first a separate being, then a progress in one stage of existence, then a transition to another stage, and so onward.

That the portion of spirit which becomes a man is born with him, grows with his growth, and is in fact himself, in a condition in which he is perceptible to the senses of other men, and therefore to them a material being.

Finally, that the spirit thus matured is not again absorbed into the mass, but, when the body drops away from it, preserves its individuality, and as a soul of psychical being becomes a conscious denizen of the subsensible universe that encompasses and pervades the material.

This exposition constitutes the philosophical basis of modern spiritualism, protean as its phenomena are, and varied as are its intellectual aspects. It is not my intention here, however, to enter upon elaborate criticism of these postulates—further than to remark that no good reason exists for exempting psychic phenomena from the law of the correlation of forces; and that, if psychological and physiological investigations exhibit one tendency more than another, it is to establish the correlation of vital and psychical phenomena. "Life," says M. Alphonse de Candolle,[1] in a definition that is in rigid accord with the facts of physiology, "is the transformation of physical motion into plastic or nervous motion." All animal tissues are endowed with force (life) peculiar to themselves.

Nor would it be candid to object to them, on the

---

[1] It is curiously interesting to trace step by step the progressive attempts of thinkers to give a comprehensive definition of life. Among the ancients the soul is the life-principle. Hegel's idea was that of the infinite potentiality expressing itself in individual form; and with Kant life is self-aim. Schelling, a greater than Hegel in some respects, leaves the question of the potential an open one, and says that life is the tendency to individuation—a metaphysical synonym for Spencer's law of differentiation. Then comes Cuvier's strictly physiological view of the case: "*Dans chaque être, la vie est un ensemble qui résulte de l'action et de la réaction mutuelle de toutes ses parties.*" Then the later definition: "*La vie est l'ensemble des fonctions qui résistent à la mort.*" Until recently these definitions have been accepted without criticism. Lawrence, of some note in England early in the present century, says, "Life is the assemblage of all the functions, and the general result of their exercise." Says Dr. Whewell, "Life is the system of vital functions." Says Herbert Spencer, with the special turning-point of the synthetic philosophy in view, "Life is the continuous adjustment of internal relations to external relations." M. de Candolle's definition occurs in his "History of the Sciences," p. 457, as a general summing up of the results of physiological investigation. All these definitions have the merit of explaining one aspect of the subject. Why not say also that life is the correlation of material forces into psychical forces? which would express the fundamental property of organism.

score that they represent merely an attenuated form of materialism; for, in the nature of things, tethered as all our thinking is to material symbols, it is impossible to think of spirit, except in the terms of subsensible matter. I am conscious of myself as force, but, when I wish to express that consciousness, I find myself inexorably tied to symbols originating in the material, and involving the notion of extension. It is true that body is a thing extended, and mind a thing that thinks; but so interwoven with all moods of consciousness is the antithesis of subject and object, that I can find no symbol to represent the ultimate reality in which the two are united, and in which I am conscious of participating. To blame the exponents of spiritualism, therefore, because they have not transcended material symbols in the literature of the subject, is to blame them because they have not effected the impossible—the impossible even to Hegel, whose monologues of talk, sighed forth by starts in a noiseless voice (as Heyne paradoxically expresses it), would have supplied a new series of symbols, had it been possible.

Again, that in their hands the transcendental often degenerates into twaddle only proves the intimate relation that subsists between the two—a relation that no philosopher thoroughly escapes.

Few minds possess the pictorial energy adequate to the task of visualizing the invisible, and this is what the literature of spiritualism practically attempts, only to fall into a series of paradoxes in which bodiless body appears as the habitual definition of spirit: so impossible is it to disconnect our most intangible fancies from the idea of extension.

I am tethered to matter as to a pivot. I may walk round and round, and round and round my tether in a circle, till I drop dead by the way, but can never snap the invisible thread that binds me to the centre and belittles my most discursive moods. Yet more: when I drop dead of weariness, I return to matter, the silent cemetery of man. It begets me—devours me. Yet I defy it, and insist, with the idealist, that it is a fancy of mine.

Our little lives are thus likened to hours in the turret of Notre-Dame. I remember as if it had been but yesterday, though years have passed since then, the sunny Parisian afternoon when I slipped through a little door into twilight, and toiled up the three-hundred and eighty-nine steps that lead to the dizzy gallery supported by slender columns. The slanting sun shot yellow beams through thin slits in the wall. Then came two hundred steps in the dark; then I suddenly emerged into a little four-square world, half-way between Paris and heaven. Its people were apes with the bosoms of women and the brawny hands and arms of men, dogs and bears, and elephants and goats, and devils as huge as Hercules, with the scaly backs of dragons and the knotted muscles of gladiators—their faces prolonged into beaks or snouts, as suited the whim of their creator. I remember one terrible bird, half eagle, half macaw, that had its hideous head smothered in drapery, like an old woman's in the rain.

I never think of that afternoon in the turret of Notre-Dame, without likening it to life, and the Paris far beneath, girt with its ribbon of a river, to the subsensible world that Prof. Tyndall talks about. From the dark you emerge into it, with its dragons and *gargouilles*. The hum of a (to you) subsensible world comes up from beneath. Lastly, you can only escape by dropping down into the dark. So with life.

What wonder, then, if like Epimenides men fall into mystic trances, and insist that they talk with spirits? Conscious of being something, yet suspended by a hair over the bottomless pit of nothingness, knowing that the hair must snap asunder to-day or to-morrow, on the third day at the latest, the man who can drink his weird and make no moan is braver than most men are, whatever his disloyalty to the supernal.

The sphinx of matter has nothing to say as to the problem of destiny that keeps mankind so ill at ease, nor any thing to say of man, save that—

> "He is he knows not what,
> He comes he knows not whence;
> His whither knows he not,
> Save that he passes hence."

Four baffling silences! The hold of spiritualism on the minds of thoughtful men is thus due to the fact that it assumes to solve these problems of being and destiny, that vex a man the more the more he thinks, by actual experiment, and to verify experimentally that which has hitherto been accepted as a mystery.

I have dwelt by way of introduction on the philosophical and religious aspects of the subject, because spiritualism assumes to be a philosophy and a religion, resting solidly on psychical phenomena demonstrative of the reality of psychical beings and of a psychic universe interpenetrating and pervading the material. Its mediums are its priests—its prophets—its revealers. It assumes as a necessary postulate that by-and-by, in the process of evolution, will come, as the product of human progress and as its ultimate result, a man so psychical in structure as to live *en rapport* with the subsensible world. It is urged, in support of this view, that man is becoming more and more nervous, and more and more psychical, as evolution proceeds and centuries pass. It is a cardinal principle of the system that the medium possesses and represents in varying intensity this higher psychical organization, and that, by virtue of this possession, he is the revealer of the psychic universe; and its exponents point to the phenomena as evidences of the authenticity of his pretensions. If they are susceptible of explanation without calling upon the denizens of another world, and upon physiological principles, then the pretensions of spiritualism are destitute of proper foundation. But let it be finally conceded that, although there has been no little jugglery mixed with them, by men anxious to turn a penny with *séances*, the phenomena have been subjected to rigid scientific scrutiny, and constitute, at least, valuable additions to the verified facts of psychology. On the other hand, while the scientific frankly concede the authenticity of the phenomena, strange as they are, it will, I apprehend, become the exponents of spiritualism to own that, considered as a philosophy or as a religious system, or as contributions to either, the speculations and revelations of professed mediums are of no value whatever.

This by way of introduction. In what follows I shall limit myself to the scientific aspects of the phenomena, leaving generalizations to the fancy of the reader.

II.

METHOD OF INVESTIGATION, AND SUMMARY OF CONCLUSIONS.

I WAS a boy of sixteen when, in the winter of 1856–'57, the first wave of spiritualism swept over the little town of Stafford, Connecticut, now one of its New-England centres of activity. Mediums had occasionally dropped in and run brief careers previous to that date. Among them was Mr. Home, a native of Lebanon, Conn., whose romantic career in Europe has since attracted considerable attention, and with whom the tests of Prof. Crookes have been mainly conducted. He was in those days a local celebrity, and journeyed from town to town, giving *séances*. I remember him as a tall, heavy-faced, awkward, reddish-haired stripling of from twenty to twenty-five years of age, with the lost expression of countenance that physicians ordinarily associate with the epileptic malady; and at several of his *séances* I was present.

When, in 1864, I became a resident of New York City, it devolved on me, as the representative of a daily newspaper, to study the phenomena as illustrated at Metropolitan Hall, in Sixth Avenue, and afterward at Dodworth Hall, in Broadway, as well as to attend all private *séances* at which admission was attainable. The first result of this practice, attended with every possible device to detect imposition, was naturally a somewhat critical familiarity, not only with the *personnel* of mediums themselves, but with the mental aura of trance, clairvoyance, and the kindred sensorial phenomena. Secondly, after duly testing the more remarkable feats of Mr. C. H. Foster, and other celebrated mediums, in every available manner, I was reluctantly forced to dismiss one scientific explanation after another, as inadequate to the facts, and either to suspend opinion, or to cast about for an explanation, both adequate to the phenomena and rigidly scientific in its terms. Phantom hands writing messages with Faber's pencils, under conditions in which deception is impossible, are somewhat different from the clever manipulations of a Blitz or a Houdin; and I have seen them come slowly out of nothingness in my own room, pick up a pencil, scribble a message in very legible handwriting, and dissolve into nothingness again, leaving the pencil as quiet as it was before. I have seen a pencil write without hands on my own table, and subscribe initials at the end; but it has been the phenomena of writing, not the messages, that have been of value.

I was very particular in testing the question whether these phenomena were merely illusive—

a phantasmagoria of the senses—having frequently witnessed the phenomenon at mesmeric *séances*, of that kind of psychic control that enables the operator to impress illusions at will upon the senses of his subject. I was accordingly careful to note that no drowsiness nor nervous shock on my part preceded the phantom appearances; also, not to permit my attention to be fixed upon any one article in the room, and to avoid personal contact with the medium previous to the exhibition. These precautions are more important than they at first appear; for many facts, both experimental and observed, have convinced me that the semi-mesmeric state is more easily induced than most scientific observers are aware. For example, a person who will fix his eyes on an object at an angle above them, without elevating his face accordingly, and retain them in that position, may induce an unconquerable drowsiness in from four to six minutes; while, to fix the eyes in the same manner on an object on the level with them, produces the phenomenon with far less rapidity. Part of the result in the first instance is, therefore, due to the physiological action on the optic nerves and ganglia, of lifting the eyes at an unnatural angle, and retaining them fixedly in that position. Indeed, in many persons that I have experimented with as to this point, the phenomenon of trance rapidly supervenes with the eyes in this position, and in every instance a state bordering upon somnambulism has been induced. It is a curious fact, too, that no other unnatural position of the eyes has this physiological effect; although passing the tips of the fingers slowly and rhythmically across velvet induces an analogous drowsiness.

Thus, taking every possible precaution to avoid those nervous states in which illusions spring up naturally, or are easily imposed upon the senses, I was soon able to state authoritatively that the phenomena are not phantasmagorial, or mere imaginings, incident to an unnatural nervous or cerebral state, but actual objective existences—real to the senses, real as matters of fact. The theory that the phenomena are due to conscious or unconscious cerebral action, unless cerebral action is competent to lift heavy bodies without hands, though it applies to a considerable series of the facts, breaks down in view of the more important series. Morbid cerebral action may cause its victim to see phantoms, but it cannot endow him with the power to make others see them. Nevertheless, there is a great deal of unconscious cerebration interwoven with the phenomena of spiritualism.

I shall not stop to discuss either of these theories, further than to say that they break down under practical tests.

The experimental and observational investigations into the nature and physiology of mesmeric phenomena were, however, though the psychological theory did break down, of value in one important particular: as they led to a careful study of the literature of the subject and a careful examination of the phenomena in common between mesmerism and spiritualism. One of these, namely, clairvoyance, in some of its aspects, is the pivot and centre of the psychical states associated with spiritualism as well as of those associated with mesmerism; and to the physiology of this state—for there is no psychical phenomenon without its physiological exponents —it seemed to me worth the while to direct my attention. It might or might not furnish the clew to the production of the phantom phenomena, of which Prof. Crookes has since recorded very full memoranda; but, whether it did or did not, its results would contribute somewhat to the stock of physiological observation.

But the investigation gradually enlarged and opened new vistas, finally extending itself further and further into the domain of medical psychology, with observations from life of morbid psychical states and of their physiological causes, microscopic studies of nervous tissue and of cerebral structure, and experimental inquiries as to the functions of the various nerve-centres.

I was led in this direction, from finding that clairvoyance is often the psychological exponent of a certain morbid nervous condition, and with a view to ascertain whether it is ever dissociated from nervous perversion. This, of course, eventuated in my gathering as many memoranda from life as possible, of instances in which clairvoyance and its associate states were confessedly morbid, with a view to compare symptoms and note points of difference. I commenced these special studies in the summer of 1868, and have since pursued them in the interstices of work as a journalist and contributor to scientific literature—with what result scientific men must judge.

My own observations of spiritualism since that period, with an eye sharpened by long study of nervous disturbances, have convinced me of three things: First, that its phenomena are invariably associated with nervous and generally with mental perversion, and that the moral aberrations and morbid impulses associated with mediums are the exponents of that perversion; secondly, that mediums, as a rule, particularly those addicted to trance, are persons of defective physical organization; thirdly, that the *séances* rapidly exhaust the nervous energies of the operator. I have notes of one instance in which the medium died of the exhaustion consequent upon his most celebrated feat, that of tearing an iron sink, incorporated into the solid masonry of a wall, from its moorings, by simply placing his hand upon the edge of it. Mr. Benjamin Hawkes, of Liverpool, England, a medium of some celebrity, fell dead under circumstances somewhat similar in the autumn of 1873, and, notwithstanding his magnificent *physique*, Mr. Home is an invalid at forty. So with Miss Kate Fox. Mr. J. R. Brown develops symptoms of exceeding physical exhaustion when his *séances* are at all prolonged, or call for more than ordinary feats.

Again, in *séances* given by trance-mediums, I have observed that those significant prodromata of the fit in its ordinary aspects, sudden cadaverous pallor, a kind of fading of the eye, accompanied with dilatation of the pupil, and a slight nervous shock, invariably precede and announce the supervention of the trance. In table-tipping this shock occasions the slight tremor of the table before the manifestations occur, and is frequently visible in slight convulsive jerkings of the medium's hands. The same shock precedes the supervention of the mesmeric trance.

Another fact that I regard as conclusively established is that, although the trance supervenes at the will of the operator, it must always be preceded by a stage of incubation more or less prolonged, during which nervous hebetude is distinctly present, the operator is more or less taciturn and irritable, and the intellectual faculties are torpid.

I once attended a series of *séances* given by a celebrated trance-medium, who insisted that my head was surrounded by a halo running through the whole spectrum of colors, that I had traveled for years in Syria, talked with the Arab in his tent, and whiffed my cigar with the Jew in his native Jerusalem: not a word of which had any justification in fact, save a somewhat minute acquaintance with the Semitic languages and their literature, and a fervid sympathy with the type of mysticism the literature illustrates.

This instance is a type of many. Indeed, in its more ordinary aspects, the mental impressions in clairvoyance invariably consist of the two elements, nervous perception and cerebration, in the same manner as impressions received through the media of the senses; the only difference consisting in the fact that the former originate in a peripheral nervous aura. I shall not attempt to say that all the trances of spiritual mediums are so limited in their manner of receiving impressions—for I am satisfied, from personal observation and from physiological study, that there is a higher type of trance, that has its origin in the gray matter of the brain, and is more immediate in its processes. This, however, is but a cerebral stage of the same type of nervous perversion, and will be adverted to again by-and-by. What I wish to impress on the reader's mind at this juncture is, that the peripheral aura, that produces the sensory phenomena of clairvoyance, independent of the media of the senses, is a symptom of nervous degeneracy; that—to employ a medical term—it is an exponent of neurosis.

Comparing, then, the series of psychical phenomena upon which spiritualism rests with the more pronounced series familiar to medical psychologists, from Esquirol to Maudsley and other living masters, the first observation of the student will be that a singular parallelism exists between the two series; that trance is the exponent of the latter equally with the former, and that the physical precursors of the trance incident to the latter series are invariably present in the former. If he is of an inquiring turn of mind, he will, at this stage, furnish himself with a microscope, and make a thorough study of nervous tissue, then address himself to the careful investigation of function. He will put himself to the pains to investigate the various phases of morbid function, particularly as relates to the nerve-centres, remembering always that one fact is worth fifty clever but unverified hypotheses, and that it is not advisable to have an opinion at all, unless the facts not only warrant but command it. Having pursued this course for a few years, he is competent to investigate the nature and relations of morbid psychical phenomena, and will long mightily to dissect the cerebral and nervous organism of a spiritual medium, by way of determining its pathological condition.

The point I wish to impress is, that of the three kindred groups of phenomena—that pertaining to mesmerism, the more pronounced group incident to spiritualism, and the still more interesting series illustrated in morbid psychology—it is impossible thoroughly to investigate the middle series without examining the other two with equal thoroughness. It was his accurate and extensive acquaintance with morbid psychology, amassed by years of practical contact with nervous disorders, that enabled Dr. Maudsley, with unerring sagacity, to diagnose epilepsy as the cause of the trances of Swedenborg, and finally to collect and sift the facts of his visit to London in a manner to demonstrate the diagnosis.

Prof. Crookes and Mr. A. R. Wallace—the one not a physiologist, the other more attentive to structure than to function—have erred, therefore, it seems to me, in having pursued an incorrect method of investigation, and in neglecting to subject the physiological traits of mediums to the minutest scrutiny. The true method seems to me to be obvious. Here are so many persons—one in a thousand possibly—who are competent to produce certain phenomena. They are not persons of superior organization, physical or cerebral. Some of them, indeed, are of very low type physically and intellectually. The question for scientific inquiry, then, is not whether these phenomena involve the presumption of superhuman intervention, but by what perversion of nervous function the medium is enabled to produce them.

Now, to answer the conditions of the problem as a scientific one, any proposed explanation of the phenomena must put order of sequence and relation into the facts, protean as they are. It must demonstrate the agency by which they are produced, and indicate the special perversion of nervous function concerned in their production. Finally, it must lie within the circle of verifiable hypotheses, which, unfortunately, is not the case with the psychic-force theory—a beautiful but romantic dream, having no relation to the demonstrated laws of physics and physiology.

In accordance with this method of investigation, the phenomena appear to me to present two very distinct series, seldom present in the same person, which I shall style respectively nervo-psychic and nervo-dynamic—meaning, under the former, to include clairvoyance in its ordinary aspects, trance, prevision, presentiment, and the like; under the latter, table-tipping, rappings, levitation of bodies, writing with phantom-hands, production of visible phantoms from luminous clouds, and other feats involving the presumption of an invisible dynamic agency. That both series have the same etiology my memoranda of cases will, I think, show beyond reasonable doubt.

I have thus briefly indicated my own course of studies, pursued somewhat fitfully for the last ten years, and the method of investigation to which they have led, by way of preface to a series of conclusions that I shall state first, and verify afterward:

1. That there is no pathological difference between the trances of mediums, the induced trances of mesmerism, and the trances incident to epileptic and cataleptic attacks; the three types equally involving reflex excitability of the gray matter of the brain, during partial suspension of the motor centres and, in catalepsy, of the medullary centres. The same sudden pallor and perceptible fading of the eye, with slight nervous shock, precede the super-

vention of the fit, and the same exponent of heat in the coronal region of the cranium is more or less developed in all cases.

2. That spirit-seeing, as illustrated in the cases of Judge Edmonds, A. J. Davis, Mrs. Woodhull, and mediums of that class, is a well-marked symptom of a single type of nervous and cerebral lesion; which lesion is accompanied by a mental aura, distinguished by a vague, generalizing tendency, and by morbid sensorial impressions, such as those of which the literature of spiritualism largely consists.

3. That this lesion develops as one of its exponents a peculiar sensory and motor aura (or atmosphere), which, entering into intimate molecular relations and contact with surrounding objects within a circle of greater or less periphery, eventuates in the phenomenon of clairvoyance in cephalic, and of table-tipping, rappings, and the like, in vital temperaments. This law is constant and invariable. The nervo-dynamic series occur only in connection with mediums of strong vital temperament; the nervo-psychic mainly in connection with mediums in whom the cerebral predominates, and both in cases where the cerebral and the vital are more or less evenly balanced, but whose manifestations are extraordinary in neither.

4. That this aura is of nervous origin, and consequent upon molecular disturbance of the nerve-centres developed by nervous disorder. That, as

such, it is more or less subject to the volition of the medium.

5. That, in its motor aspect, this nervous atmosphere is correlated with light, and susceptible of transformation into luminous clouds, into spectral apparitions, and other objective phenomena; and that the production of these phenomena constitutes a problem in nervo-molecular physics, to be investigated carefully, but having no ascertained relation to the higher spiritual aspects of human life.

6. That in its sensory aspects it enters into intimate relations with nervous organisms surrounding it, is impressed with their thoughts at greater or less distance, transmits what they know or remember to the brain of the medium, and renders the organism whence it proceeds *en rapport* with the minds of persons within the circle of its operations.

7. That both groups of phenomena are, therefore, morbid nervous phenomena, having their cause in nervous lesion, and their physiological basis in reflex excitability of the nerve-centres.

8. That, therefore, there is no occasion to refer them to the operations of an hypothetical psychic force, nor to the intervention or agency of departed spirits.

I state these propositions in detail before entering upon memoranda of cases, in order that the reader may be enabled to apply them in the less important instances, without special explanation. As Prof. Crookes remarks, it is obvious that a medium possesses something that is not possessed by ordinary men. Neither is it disputed, by those who have observed the phenomena, that, under certain conditions and within a limited distance from certain persons of special nervous organization, a force operates by which, without muscular contact, action at a distance is caused, and visible motions and audible sounds are produced in solid substances. As this force acts intelligently, Prof. Crookes and Sergeant Cox style it psychic force—or soul-force —and identify it with a psychic organism supposed to pervade and inhabit the material. Hence, in their terminology, a medium is designated as a *psychic*.

Although this theory constitutes the scientific basis of spiritualism, a man may nevertheless accept it, without accepting the cardinal tenet of the spiritualists, that the psychic is *en rapport* with the spirits of the dead. It is, on the other hand, illogical and fragmentary to accept the latter and deny the former.

Scientific progress—so far from tending to overturn a real religious faith—is gradually gathering the materials, the generalizations, let me say, for profounder conceptions of life and destiny, of religion in the larger acceptation of the word, than the last century had. The great law of the correlation of forces—the same force always present in Nature, now actual, now potential, now heat, now light, now electricity, now nervous force, now mental, but the same in all its transformations—opens new vistas for metaphysical dreamers. Alone, disconnected from phenomena, of itself only, what is the substratum of this tremendous and universal energy? This is the problem upon which, in its different aspects, every scientist labors—to the solution of which every discovery tends. Analytically, it is a mere problem of molecular physics; synthetically, it dips deep into the question of life and destiny; and though, in the strictly empirical work of the experimentalist, the idea of teleology is excluded from science, yet in the hands of men like Herbert Spencer its teleological aspects have already assumed some prominence, and will presently eventuate in a new era of profoundly speculative inquiry. So this law of correlation, to the true thinker, asks, "What is the real?" No dreaming metaphysician, with his dialect of terms for airy nothings, ever put the question more pertinently or more directly; and the psychic-force theory, it seems to me, while at war with the deeper aspects of this, according to Faraday, the highest law in physical science, fails to answer the important question in a manner that commends itself to men of real scientific aptitude, and stultifies the tendency to deeper religious conceptions, now beginning to be felt as an active force in scientific thought.

It is no doubt true, and can be established from careful comparison of ancient forms of civilization with modern, and of ancient types of the human race with modern, that there has been a general progress toward more psychical types of organization, involving a greater complexity of emotional and intellectual life. The question is, whether the average spiritual medium is an earnest of the advanced type potential in the existing; and this question can only be answered by rigid physiological investigation.

III.

CASES OF NERVO-PSYCHIC PHENOMENA.

This group includes a series of cases in which the psychic element is predominant, with notes by the way, when necessary, and is selected with a view to cover the psychological phenomena associated with spiritualism—first, with reference to their etiology, and, secondly, with reference to their nature and physiological exponents. In all instances not resting on accredited medical testimony, the facts have been carefully verified, and in the majority of instances they are stated on personal observation.

Case I.—This case is, in many respects, analogous to that of Angélique Cottin, of popular notoriety in France about the year 1850, and described at length by Robert Dale Owen, in an article entitled "The Electric Girl of La Perrière," printed in the *Atlantic Monthly* for September, 1864. Though the dynamic element predominates, yet its important psychical aspects entitle it to a place in the nervo-psychic series.

Mary Carrick, an Irish girl, eighteen years of age, very ignorant, came to this country in May,

1867. Had been subject to fits of somnambulism. Immediately upon her arrival she was engaged as a servant in a very respectable family in a large New-England town, appeared to be in good health, and performed the duties required of her in a satisfactory manner. She seldom left the house, and was totally unacquainted with the subject of spiritualism.

She had lived in this family about six weeks, when, on the 3d day of July, 1867, the bells communicating with the outside door and with the various apartments in the house commenced ringing unaccountably. The phenomenon was at first attributed to rats tampering with the wires, but examination proved this to be impossible. The bells were next isolated, but the ringing did not cease. They hung near the ceiling in the room where Mary worked, and were fully ten feet from the floor, and never rang unless the girl was in the room or in the apartment adjoining, but were often seen to be agitated and heard to ring when different members of the family were present. The ringing did not consist of a single stroke of one or more of the bells, but was the consequence of a violent agitation of them all, as if shaken by a sudden gust of wind.

A few days after this commenced, frequent loud and startling raps, on the walls, doors, or windows of the room where Mary worked, began to be heard. These noises were similar to those ordinarily produced by a smart tap of the knuckles on an article of wood, and were heard by all the members of the family and many others. They increased in frequency from day to day, until the girl became excited and at night raved in her sleep, and followed her from room to room. On several occasions they were heard at night in her bedroom, and, upon going there, it was ascertained that she was sound asleep.

About three weeks later, a series of still more extraordinary phenomena commenced. Sofas were upset, crockery fell to the floor, tables lifted and moved about the room, cooking-utensils were hurled from one point to another. No special record of these occurrences was kept for some days; but at length a journal of observations was instituted.

August 5th.—As Mary was washing, a low table, laden with two large tubs of water, was suddenly moved; and the lid of the wash-boiler, which was a copper one, was repeatedly lifted and dropped when the girl was at some distance from it. These phenomena were observed by several members of the family.

August 6th.—As Mary was ironing, the table was repeatedly lifted. Upon taking her work to another table, the phenomenon was repeated, and her flat-iron, which she left for a moment, was thrown to the floor. The table was lifted in this way at moments when she was several feet from it, and when laden with a weight of several hundred pounds. The cover of the wood-box and that of the wash-boiler were also constantly slamming; and a heavy soapstone-slab, weighing forty pounds, which formed the top of a case of drawers, was repeatedly lifted and dropped. On the afternoon of the same day, as the girl was putting away the tea-things, and about to place a metallic tray filled with dishes upon this slab, it was suddenly lifted, and knocked the tray from her hands. This was witnessed by the family, and frequently occurred afterward.

August 20*th.*—The table movements occurred frequently, and a large basket filled with clothes was hurled to the floor. A small board, used for scouring knives, was also thrown across the room, and the doors were constantly slammed.

August 25*th.*—The soapstone-slab was lifted repeatedly within an hour. At last it suddenly lifted, fell with great force, and was broken in two through the middle, Mary being in the act of wringing out the dishcloth. A few minutes later one-half of the broken slab was thrown to the floor and dashed in pieces. This stone, it should be added, had a few days before been taken from its place and laid upon the floor in an adjoining room, with a heavy bucket upon it; but, as the movements were not abated, it was replaced and fastened down with strong wooden clamps, which were forcibly torn away. Another soapstone-slab, in which the copper boiler was set, and which had become loosened from the brickwork, was split and thrown to the floor in a similar manner. A fragment of it was also hurled from the wash-room to the room adjoining. A wooden table standing against the wall often started out into the room, and was on one occasion upset.

August 26*th* and 27*th*.—The rappings were particularly frequent and vigorous; movables were thrown about, and a large wash-tub, filled with clothes soaking, was hurled from the wash-form to the floor and upset. A stool, having a pail of water on it, moved along the floor, and a porcelain kettle was lifted and dropped. The furniture in the room was also considerably agitated. On the evening of August 27th the girl was sent away for two days, and the manifestations ceased.

August 29*th*.—Mary returned, and reported that she had not been troubled during her absence; but, within two hours after, the demonstrations commenced again and continued for two weeks.

September 12*th*.—A violent hysteriform attack supervened and lasted for two hours, during which the girl was unconscious and could be restrained only by the united strength of several attendants. The paroxysm subsiding, she slept quietly till morning. The paroxysms recurred at intervals of two days, but without loss of consciousness, and were marked by no peculiar symptoms, except a distressing sensation at the base of the brain. She also complained that she heard strange noises, and became subject to severe paroxysms of bleeding at the nose.

September 18*th*.—The girl was sent to the asylum,

no rappings or other phenomena having occurred since the date of the first hysteriform fit.

At the end of the third week she was pronounced able to resume her work, and returned in a very happy frame of mind, though subject to sudden starts. But the phenomena did not occur again, and she continued comparatively calm for nearly two months, grew very fleshy, and was learning to read and write with considerable rapidity.

November 28*th*.—At night an attack of somnambulism supervened; she got up and dressed herself, went to the room of her mistress, and asked permission to clean the windows. She remembered nothing of this in the morning. These paroxysms occurred nightly for five consecutive nights, when they were replaced by hysteriform attacks, occurring periodically at the same hour. She was again removed to the asylum, where she was afterward employed as house-maid.

Certain symptoms worth noting accompanied the phenomena in their later stages, among them attacks of lethargy bordering on trance. Loud playing on the organ made her so sleepy that slumber soon supervened; but so long as the playing was soft she was wakeful. At night in her sleep she would sing for hours, although she had never been heard to sing in the daytime.

It should be added, also, that soon after her somnambulism developed itself she became clairvoyant. One remarkable instance of her clairvoyance was verified. She declared that a young lady, one of the members of the family, then on a visit to a distant city, was very sick, and was exceedingly distressed about it, notwithstanding the assurance of the family that the young lady had just been heard from and was quite well. She would not be comforted, however, and still declared that the absent lady was very ill and suffered extremely from a bad sore on her hand. This afterward proved to be exactly as she had stated.

In this remarkable case several points, aside from its general bearing, should be noted particularly.

In the first place, the phenomena were noticed to occur at moments when the girl was engaged in heavy work, calling for considerable outlay of physical strength, and a corresponding emphasis of volition. The soapstone-slab was broken, for example, while she was wringing out the dishcloth.

Secondly, at a later stage of the disorder they were replaced by hysteriform attacks, while the latter were finally replaced by fits of somnambulism and by the half-trance of clairvoyance.

Thirdly, these attacks had the stated periodicity incident to epileptic paroxysms, of which somnambulism is frequently the precursor.

Fourthly, in common with lesions involving trance, pains and soreness at the base of the brain indicated disorder of the medullary centres.

CASE II.—D. C. Densmore, of Boston, Mass., by profession a sea-captain, became subject in 1822 to the consciousness of being attended in all his movements by invisible intelligences, which assisted him at crises in his studies and business. Frequently, when in doubt as to what course to pursue, he has been directed by a voice that speaks in distinct words, as one man would speak to another. At a later period he became subject to attacks, during which he wrote automatically, and this was soon followed by clairvoyance, and by the gift of healing by the laying on of hands. This power of healing seemed to be wholly independent of volition. He gives many verifiable instances of cures worked in this way, and believes that the gift emanates from spirit-guides having control of his organism.

In 1843–'44, Mr. Densmore was master of the ship Massasoit, of Bath, Maine, on a whaling-voyage to the South Atlantic and Indian Oceans, and on his passage home arrived on the coast February 1, 1844. Deciding to pass between Nantucket and the Georges shoals, to save pilotage through the Vineyard Sound, and having made only twenty-four miles northing for the whole month of February, owing to constant gales from the northeast, he found the ship one day at noon in nine fathoms of water, and drifting directly on the shoals. As the water lessened about a fathom a mile, and they were drifting a mile an hour, he concluded that the vessel must strike about four o'clock that afternoon. He had made several ineffectual attempts to head the ship round, so as to drift parallel with the shoals, and had lost all his available head-sails, excepting an old fore-staysail, with which and the weather-clew of the reefed foresail he hoped to succeed; but the former was scarcely hoisted when it went into ribbons, the latter following. This baffled the last hope of being able to tack about, and there was nothing but to wait for doom, which, unless the wind shifted, was sure and soon.

Captain Densmore retained the lead in his possession, now and then taking the depth of water, and kept the officers and crew in ignorance of the real state of affairs, in order to prevent demoralization and save the ship if an opportunity should be offered. At a little past three o'clock the cast of the lead showed six fathoms of water, and Captain Densmore went to his cabin, trying, he says, to feel very solemn, but quite unable to appreciate the situation. There he sat and thought for a few minutes, and finally determined to advise the officers and crew of the danger, as the minutes were not many between them and death. He went on deck, never calmer in his life, and was just about to tell the officers how imminent the peril was, when a voice, distinct above the raging elements, said:

"Wear ship."

He immediately answered, as though a human voice had spoken to him:

"I can't wear ship; I haven't any sails."

"Make a sail of the men; man the weather fore-rigging with the men," was the mysterious answer.

The practicability of doing so flashed upon him in an instant, and, instead of setting the men to praying, he called them aft, told them what he wanted in a few words, and they all scampered forward, joking at being made into a storm-sail. The captain now lashed himself to the wheel, and, as soon as the men were all in the rigging, rolled the wheel hard up, when the ship began to fall off, and in a few minutes had fairly headed about. Neither wind nor sea abated at all until after seven o'clock.

Captain Densmore attributes the saving of the ship and of the lives of thirty-four men wholly to the interposition of the voice that he habitually hears at such crises.

He has heard these voices frequently, but only on occasions of imminent peril.

For example, on another occasion, when making the passage of the South Atlantic, the ship got short of provisions, and they were making the most of every breath of wind to get home. One night, after a scanty supper, Captain Densmore went on deck, the ship making not more than two knots an hour, and the sea as smooth as a pond. He sauntered along the waist of the ship, and stood leaning on the weather-rail. Directly he heard a voice say:

"Take in sail."

Captain Densmore scanned the horizon low down and overhead, but not a cloud was visible. The sun was just setting.

He felt uneasy and wanted to follow the prompting of the voice, but could find no excuse for doing so, and did not wish to tell the mate his only reason for such a proceeding; as they were using the utmost available expedition to shorten the distance between them and home, and the officers and men would certainly regard him as insane to give an order that would cause needless delay.

He leaned over the weather-rail and scanned the sunset until the lurid disk had dipped beneath the sea. Presently, brassy streaks shot up beyond the horizon higher and higher, as the sun dropped lower down. Captain Densmore turned and looked to leeward, and noticed that the brassy haze had already crept all along the lee-horizon. On this he decided, and told the mate to call up the men and take in sail. The mate went forward, growling. "Hadn't you better send down the top-gallant yards and masts?" slurred the old salt in undertone, but he obeyed. "Is the old man crazy?" grumbled the men, but they, too, obeyed.

Scarcely had all the light sails been furled, the courses clewed up, and the rigging hauled out preparatory to reefing, when a terrible tornado struck the ship, and the masts swayed like saplings and threatened to come down. The wind struck the vessel at five in the afternoon, and for eleven hours she was almost on her beam-ends. This was off Cape Hatteras, where so many have gone down.

Another incident must suffice. One morning, about five weeks after the tornado, they sighted a full-rigged brig to windward. The wind was light, yet the brig was under close-reefed topsails. Captain Densmore went on board to procure provisions. The vessel proved to be the President, of Portland, Maine, Captain Sargent. By observation at twelve, Highland Light on Cape Cod bore west-northwest fifty-four miles; the wind was light from the northward. They were now heading off-shore. When Captain Densmore left the brig, Captain Sargent asked which way he was going to stand.

"In-shore," answered Captain Densmore.

"Then you'll be ashore on Cape Cod in less than twenty-four hours," replied Sargent. "Stand off! There's going to be a terrible northeaster; I've been looking for it for two days, and now the indications are that it will be here before night."

And, to make his argument more effective: "I have been in the West India trade twenty-two years, at all seasons of the year, and have never lost a studding-sail boom."

As Captain Sargent was an experienced pilot on the coast, Densmore concluded to follow his advice, and gave the order to brace forward and stand off-shore; but scarcely had it been executed, when he heard a voice say distinctly:

"Tack ship."

He obeyed without a moment's hesitation and headed directly for Cape Cod; but, as they neared the land, at 4 P. M., the wind veered round, and the next morning they passed Seguin Light at the entrance of the Kennebec River. The President was blown twice to the southward of the gulf, and, after six weeks' beating about, finally went ashore on Monomoy Point, Cape Cod, and was lost.

It should be observed that the progress of this case presents in the course of its thirty years all the successive stages of larvated epilepsy, from its precursory consciousness of attending intelligences to clairvoyance, about which are grouped some of the most remarkable psychic phenomena known to medical men. Mr. Densmore is of cerebro-vital temperament, has been subject to nervous attacks from a boy, and inherits an epileptic predisposition.

CASE III.—Andrew Jackson Davis, born at Blooming Grove, New York, August 11, 1826, is of slender *physique* and of cephalic temperament. In 1843, at the age of seventeen, he was subjected to mesmeric experiments by William Levingston, once well known as an exponent of mesmerism. In 1844 he became subject to spontaneous attacks of trance, in one of which he lay for sixteen hours. In these cerebral attacks he converses with invisible beings, and describes the scenery and constitution of the spirit-world; but of late years his nervous system has in some degree recovered its tone, and the attacks have supervened less frequently.

CASE IV.—Mary ——, born in Paris, France, and eleven years of age June 26, 1873. Has lived in this country eight years. In conversation exhibits uncommon intensity of mental action and uncommon vividness of mental vision. In addition to her native tongue, she speaks German and English with singular fluency. For several years previous to the attack described in the following paragraphs, Mary had occasionally complained that she saw about her the forms of persons who were dead, and, as there could be no reasonable doubt of her sincerity, the fact gave her parents considerable uneasiness.

During the summer of 1873 her health appeared to be gradually failing, and one day, about the first of December, she startled her mother by telling her that she saw her dead sister Louise, who had come near her in an angel-form and told her she would make her well, so that she would never be sick any more. Her mother tried to induce her to dismiss the subject, but she seemed unable to stop talking, and kept on describing her sister, who, she said, was dressed in pure white, her face bright and shining, her hair illumined with light, and golden dew-drops dripping from her wings. She also saw her dead brother; but, while talking, her strength failed, and she sank down, as in death.

It was about ten o'clock in the morning when this apparent death occurred, but, her parents supposing she was already dead, no physician was called, and preparations were commenced for the funeral. The body was, however, kept until the following afternoon at four o'clock, when, taking a final look of the remains, the coffin-lid was sealed, and the coffin was placed in the hearse. The procession now started for the grave.

They had proceeded but a little distance when the quick ear of the mother caught the sound of a muffled but familiar cry, and she expressed a suspicion that it came from the coffin of little Mary. Her suspicion was overruled, and the procession trundled on. But in a few minutes another cry was heard. The hearse was now stopped, and the coffin withdrawn. The struggles of the supposed dead could be distinctly heard after the door of the hearse was opened, and, on opening the coffin, little Mary was found alive, having in her struggles torn away parts of her death-robe. She was taken from the coffin, conveyed home, and placed in a vinegar-bath; recovered rapidly, and was soon as well as ever.

After her recovery, she stated that she could hear and feel during her trance, but was unable to move a hand or make the slightest stir. She knew when they dressed her for the grave, when she was laid in the coffin, and heard them fasten down the lid, but was powerless to stir until she had been carried some distance in the hearse, the motion of which, slow and rhythmical, probably resuscitated her. She described, with singular enthusiasm and beauty of diction, the beatific beings she saw while entranced, and appeared, for some months, to recur to them periodically, though her parents spared no pains to divert her mind from the terrible episode.

Romantic as this case may seem to the general

reader, the scientific will discern in it a very simple and ordinary attack of catalepsy, heralded by the usual prodromata of cataleptic trance, nervous perturbation, and a consciousness of being environed by spiritual intelligences.

CASE V.—John Worth Edmonds, born in 1798, at Hudson, New York; graduated at Union College in 1816; of cephalic temperament. In 1851, after spending twenty-five years in unremitting professional work, and rising to the dignity of judge of the Supreme Court of the State of New York, his health gave way, and persistent mental depression supervened. His disorder took the form of an almost monomaniac persistency in discussing the subject of death and future destiny. In this frame of mind, and with this predisposition, he spent months in experimenting on the phenomena of spiritualism and recording his memoranda, which he afterward published in book-form.

Soon after he became a medium, while reading in bed one evening, he began to feel the intangible pressure of spirit-hands and to hear rappings. A little later he became impressed with the notion that he must call on a certain man, personally unknown to him, and receive a spiritual communication of a higher order than he had hitherto experienced. He went, and received what he firmly believed to be a message from a dead friend. He often averred that he saw spirits about him while he was delivering judicial decisions.

He went to Central America soon after he was developed as a medium; and the members of his circle, on his return, professing to have been kept miraculously advised of the events of his voyage, simultaneously with their occurrence, he verified their memoranda by comparing them day by day with the records of his diary. This coincidence he was accustomed to relate as proof of the soundness of his belief. Nor was this all. He was, during the same year, spiritually notified of the illness of his grandson in Canada, and of the death of his friend Isaac C. Hopper. He foretold the destruction of the ill-fated steamer Henry Clay, and was frequently warned against perfidious associates and advised of impending evils. His daughter also became a medium, delivering messages in languages of which she professed to know nothing out of the trance-state.

"My father had been dead thirty-six years," says the judge, describing one of his midnight visions, "and he and Mr. Van Buren had been friends for life. When I first saw their spirits, my father was standing in the middle of the room, on my left. He had an alert look, and was very easy and unconstrained in his attitude. Mr. Van Buren stood against the wall on my right, near me, and six or eight paces from my father. He had a puzzled look, as if he did not exactly comprehend his condition. He knew me and my father—knew that my father was dead, that he also was dead, and that I was not. I did not observe what first took place between them. My attention was first particularly attracted to them by hearing Mr. Van Buren say: 'I don't understand this; I know I am dead, but I am the same as I was before. I am on earth yet. There are my family, my home, my country; and the matters that interested me in life are just as near me as ever, yet removed from me. Can this be the death I have thought of so long, and is this to be my life after death forever?' This thought seemed to goad him into action. He turned to the right, and, bending down, began to pluck at something, as if removing weeds from his path; and thus he slowly worked his way from me."

Judge Edmonds wrote voluminously at this early period, with Bacon and Swedenborg, Van Buren and Washington, as his attendant spirits.

One of his latest utterances consisted of a communication from the late Judge Peckham, describing the Ville du Havre disaster.

Let the reader note that, in this case, the phenomena associated with spiritualism supervened after a considerable period of nervous depression, accompanied with indications of physical debility—the initial symptoms of a nervous disorder that rendered his after-years so many cycles of suffering, and engendered an intellectual aura, that, without perceptibly impairing his faculties, fatally determined their direction.

CASE VI.—A. B. Crandall, of slender *physique*

and cephalic temperament, states that premonitory dreams have, from boyhood, played an important part in his psychical life; but it was not until 1852 that he began to pay special attention to these phenomena. He was resident in a remote district in the West, isolated from early associations, twenty leagues from a post-office, and sixty from the nearest railway-station. Then began a series of dreams, foreshadowing the future in a manner so remarkable as to enforce his attention; and for ten years there was not a single instance in which dreaming of walking and talking with a person who had died many years before did not herald the reception of news from home. "One day," says Mr. Crandall, "meeting an old friend, who had a son on the border of the Indian Territory, he astonished me by remarking: 'Crandall, I am going to hear from James to-day, for I had a long talk with your dead brother last night, and I have never known the omen to fail me.' About three hours later the letter came."

Case VII.—This case rests upon the authority of Mr. Macnish, author of "The Philosophy of Sleep." A young man, whose father was dead, was in danger of losing a very important suit for want of evidence, proving a certain transaction on the part of his father, the papers to which had been lost. The case was to come on the following day, and, having exhausted all means of exhuming the facts he wanted, the young man went to bed in despair, and, after thinking long, fell asleep. He had just a single flash of dream, during which his father appeared standing by the bed, and told him to visit a certain barrister, who had long since given up business, but who had conducted the negotiations, and was cognizant of the whole transaction. The apparition vanished *sub umbras*, but, on visiting the old barrister the next morning, the evidence required was completed link by link, and the cause was won.

Mr. Macnish thinks the father must have told his son, at some date previous to his death, the details of the transaction, and that what he had so thoroughly forgotten as to imagine that he had never known it, must have come to him in his sleep. But in the light of facts bearing upon the important part that ante-natal impressions play in certain states of consciousness, this hypothesis is unnecessary. In certain abnormal and highly-excited states of the nervous system, as is proved by abundant facts, matters impressed upon the memory of a father present themselves to the consciousness of his posterity. I have no doubt, for instance, that the daughter of Judge Edmonds derives her capacity to speak, in the trance-state, in languages unfamiliar to her in the ordinary moods of consciousness, from her father's studies in that direction, or rather, from the nervous habit engendered by those studies—for investigation has left no question that memory is an organic record, and that every event and idea of a man's life is distinctly recorded in his nervous organism, and hence transmissible.

Case VIII.—This case illustrates the position taken in the preceding paragraph, and rests upon the authority of the London *Lancet.* Dr. F. Mayhew, of Glastonbury, England, writing to the 1873 volume of that journal, says that there is now living in a village in the vicinity of that town one Eli H——, aged seventy-five. Before he was born his father made a vow that if his wife, then pregnant, should bring him a girl, she having had three in succession, he would never speak to the baby as long as he lived. The issue was a boy; but, what is most remarkable, this boy would never speak to his father, and, during his father's lifetime, was never known to speak to anybody except his mother and his three sisters. The father died when the son was thirty-five years old, since which he has been possessed of the normal faculty of articulation.

Dr. J. W. Eastment, of Wincanton, who was born in the village where dumb Eli lived, remarks, in writing to the *Lancet,* that the afflicted father would often entreat his son to talk with him, but that neither entreaties nor threats, to say nothing of promises, were of the least avail. The father even offered him half his property, if he would but once speak to him—but all to no purpose. The mother also admonished the son, and begged him to talk to his father, but his reply invariably was: "Mother, I would talk to father if I could, but the moment he comes near me my voice begins to falter and I can't say a word."

"The facts of this case," says Dr. Mayhew, "are indeed unexplainable on ordinary principles. My appeal is to the more than ordinary acquaintance with psychological phenomena possessed by readers of the leading medical journals."

CASE IX.'—This case, of a young lady of German parentage, resident in New Haven, Connecticut, and subject to cataleptic attacks, is still more directly in point. Her parents have been residents of this country for many years. German is not and has not been spoken in the family, and the cataleptic is unacquainted with it. Yet, in her trances, she talks German habitually, and with the unhesitating facility of a native.

CASE X.—The case of the boy murderer, of

---

[1] Cases, in which abnormal nervous excitation has wholly transformed the action of the nerve-centre coördinating the muscles concerned in articulation, are by no means so uncommon as is generally supposed. July 30, 1872, Miss Margaret Kelley, until that date in apparently healthy condition, was stricken with cerebral disorder, one of the exponents of which was a total forgetfulness of English, her native tongue, and considerable fluency and command of German, which she had never studied nor heard spoken to any great extent. Several months after this stroke, Miss Kelley apparently recovered from the attack, and conversed intelligently in German, but could neither speak English nor understand it without an interpreter. The explanation of these phenomena in cerebral disorders lies, no doubt, in the fact that the nerve-centre concerned in them is situated in the left anterior lobe of the cerebrum, and hence participates in the morbid condition of the great intellectual centres grouped about it.

Boston, Jesse R. Pomeroy, known as the boy with the white eye, inexplicable as it seems, also strikingly illustrates how the nervous impressions of a father may reappear in his posterity. At periodical intervals, the boy is possessed of a morbid impulse to mutilate and torture, or cut the throats of his playmates, and has already committed several murders. His mother denies the current story that, during pregnancy, she was in the habit of going to the slaughter-house, where her husband was employed, to witness the killing of animals, or that she ever did so at all, and states that Jesse exhibited no abnormal impulses until after he was vaccinated; and, from personal examination of the case, I am inclined to credit her story so far as both assertions are concerned. It appears, from minute inquiry into the habits and antecedents of the father, that he had been subject to nervous paroxysms at different periods for many years, and that the boy, Jesse, inherited a neurotic tendency, which would, in the nature of things, have manifested itself in some form. This tendency may have been, and probably was, immediately developed by the ulceration and illness consequent upon vaccination: where the morbid tendency exists, but might lie dormant for years, it is frequently brought to the surface in this way, or by phthisis: but it descended directly from the paternal ancestor. The special direction taken by the morbid impulse in Jesse's case was, however, no doubt determined by the business in which the elder

Pomeroy was employed at and before the date of his birth, or, in other words, by the habit of mutilation, contracted by his father in the slaughter-house, which, like all habits, primarily impressed the nervous system, and was recorded in the nervous organism as a transmissible bias, to present itself in the instance of his son as a monomania, coming to the surface only in the periodical paroxysms of nervous disorder, but always existing as a latent tendency. The medical observer finds here, therefore, a singular instance of the manner in which mere customary action on the part of a progenitor recurs in the case of the son as a psychic phenomenon.

CASE XI.—Victoria Claflin, generally known as Mrs. Woodhull, native of Homer, Ohio, and born September 23, 1838; of slender *physique* and cephalic temperament; subject from girlhood to cerebral attacks (trances), in which she converses with spirits, and presents physically and psychically, with marked emphasis, the usual exponents and symptoms of larvated epilepsy. With the unmistakable mental aura incident to this type of nervous lesion, her attacks follow the more or less stated periodicity associated with it, and generally last from one to two hours, during which she talks incessantly.

At thirty years of age, at the bidding of Demosthenes, Mrs. Woodhull appeared in New York in the year 1868, and first settled at No. 17 Great Jones Street, using the clairvoyance, incident to nervous lesion of this type, as a means of support.

One dramatic incident in her career is worth repeating as an illustration of the strange mental aura, approximating to insanity, that habitually controls her. One day, while her son was very ill, she left him to make her usual round of medical visits, and on her return was startled with the tidings that the boy had been dead two hours. "No," she said, "I will not permit his death!" and with frantic energy she caught him to her bared bosom, and glided insensibly into trance, in which she remained for several hours. When she awoke, still holding the boy to her bosom, a perspiration suffused his clammy skin, and he, the supposed dead, had come back to life— and still lives in a kind of lethargy, the victim of an inherited nervous degeneration, that no skill can arrest.

In her periodical trances, and as the exponent of an advanced stage of nervous disorder, it should be observed that Mrs. Woodhull develops visibly that correlation of nerve-aura with light playing about the head so frequently noticed in larvated attacks. Indeed, in all its aspects, her case is typically illustrative of the nervous and psychical phenomena never absent, but seldom present in emphasis so marked, in mediums of the trance-class.

CASE XII.—Mrs. Russell, of Stafford, Connecticut, sees and converses with spirits, and hears nocturnal voices. Is over forty years of age, and has been subject to these phenomena for many years; of cephalic temperament, and considerably debilitated. On examination, I find that her attacks are subject to the periodicity, and present the faded eye, facial pallor, and slight *sécousses* of the muscles, incident to the cerebral type of the epileptic malady.

CASE XIII.—This case, condensed from the report of a commission of medical men, appointed to investigate and report on the nature of certain psychological phenomena associated with mesmerism, proves that epileptic convulsions may be replaced by trance, and that the latter may replace the fit so fully as to call for the periodical stage of incubation, ere repetition can supervene.

Pierre Cazot, of epileptic parentage, was received into one of the Paris hospitals, and some experiments were instituted at the instance of M. Foissac. The convulsions yielded readily to the usual passes, and Cazot was thrown into mesmeric slumber, during which, in answer to questions from members of the committee, he stated the hour and minute when his next attack would occur—which was verified to the moment. The experiments covered an interval of six months, the transformation of the convulsions into the larvated form invariably supervening under the manipulations of M. Foissac, and Cazot repeatedly foretelling the day and hour and minute when his next attack would supervene. These predictions, with a single exception, in which the variation was about five minutes, were fulfilled to the instant.

On two occasions, when M. Foissac had been introduced into the house surreptitiously, and was seated in an adjoining room, Cazot detected his presence, remarked that he was very sleepy, and was, within ten minutes, lapped in mesmeric slumber. At the last experiment, he stated to the commission that in his next attack he should be mad for days, and that after that no fits would occur; but, before the expiration of the predicted period, he was accidentally ridden down on the street, and died of the injuries received.

The committee, in reporting, detail the facts at length, but are coincident in the opinion that Cazot's prevision was limited to his disorder. It should be stated, also, that, when he emerged from the attack, he was at each experiment ascertained to have been unconscious that any questions had been put to him, or that he had uttered any predictions.

CASE XIV.—M. Cazotte, the author of "Le Diable Amoureux," was a mild and amiable man, but unfortunately infatuated with the reveries of the Illuminati. It was the year before the Revolution broke out in France, but its shadow had already fallen upon the popular consciousness, and the brassy streaks that portend the tornado were already visible low down in the horizon. La Harpe tells the story in his own dramatic way:

It was a dinner at the Academy, and a brilliant gathering of the celebrities of literature, the law, art, science, and fashion, were present—the ladies of the land among them; a splendid festival, at which ladies of the high degree of Madame de Grammont blushed not behind their fans. Condorcet and all his set were there. They sang songs, and quoted from "La Pucelle." One and one only of the assembled revelers sat apart in musing mood, and recked not the storm of jests. This was M. Cazotte, who at last, in dreamy reply to brilliant anticipations of the Revolution, then the golden age, broke in upon the tempest of talk.

"Yes, gentlemen," said Cazotte; "yes, ladies"— for a Parisian, even in the throes of prophecy, is too courteous to forget the ladies—"you will all live to see it."

"It needs no prophet's vision to see that," sneered one of the elegancies of the new intellectual era."

"Perhaps not," rejoined M. Cazotte, dreamily; "but you will, perhaps, agree that it requires more than mere guessing to tell what I am about to say to you." And, going on in his dreamy way, M. Cazotte foretells the death of those present, one after another—a dismal picture of men gashing themselves with razors, strangling themselves with nooses (any way to die); lords and ladies, and Madame de Grammont among them, riding to the guillotine in carts.

The guests laughed dismally. It was a joke, they said; but then, M. Cazotte's wit had always had an affiliation for the dismal. The host even intimated that the fun had been carried far enough; and M. Cazotte was just taking his leave, when Madame de Grammont interposed.

"But good M. Cazotte has not forecast his own destiny," said she, playfully, though with a little shudder, perhaps.

And, for reply, the prophet told the story of the Jew who walked thrice round Jerusalem.

Making all deductions for historical decoration in general, and for the attitudinizing of Celtic historians in particular, the story of M. Cazotte is typical of a class of morbid psychic phenomena seldom observed in general society, but tolerably familiar to psychological physicians. It need only be added that M. Cazotte had long been subject to periodical cerebral attacks—as, indeed, Dr. Maudsley, England's foremost alienist, has proved Swedenborg to have been, from the records of his visit to London.

CASE XV.—Emma L——, of cephalic temperament, uneducated, incapable of physical exertion, and subject to nervous disturbances, at eighteen years of age contracted the habit of inducing trance with sulphuric ether, and continued the practice until a whiff of the anæsthetic sufficed to produce the phenomenon. The experiments in this case covered an interval of two years, and were instituted by substituting mesmeric passes for the action of the drug. During the progress of these experiments Miss L—— proceeded, by regular gradations, from induced trance to clairvoyance within a circle of moderate periphery, from the latter to clairvoyance as to events and objects at varying distances, and finally to the settled interiority of spontaneous extasis, during which she seemed wholly indrawn, cataleptic rigidity often supervening.

Soon after the experiments were initiated, Miss L—— became so sensitive to the action of magnetism as to announce the presence of a large horseshoe magnet that had been placed in an adjoining room, twelve feet from the bed on which she was lying, declaring that she saw it through the wall, which was like a film between them, and indicating the exact point where it was placed. She was first tested within a moderate periphery, and was invariably correct in her answers; then at considerable distances; but, after the application of distant tests, exhibited symptoms of great exhaustion, complaining that she had been so far that it seemed as though she should never get back, and panting and sinking down with fatigue.

Her clairvoyance at large distances was verified by every available test. It was resolved, as an experiment, to send her on a trip to the moon, of which she gave a whimsical description, styling its inhabitants the little folks, explaining how they lived, that their mouths were set vertically in their faces, and painting strange pictures of lunar crags and lakes. She only saw one animal, that resembled a pig; and in one hut that she passed there was a baby in the cradle, but it was dead. They did not call it dead, however, but asleep.

On another occasion it was resolved to send her to Jupiter, but, after she had been in trance a few minutes, she showed symptoms of serious exhaustion, and it was deemed best to discontinue. In this trance she spoke of passing the land of the little folks, and of seeing them as she returned.

And now was rapidly developed the phenomenon of spontaneous trance, during the paroxysms of which she talked of the denizens of the spirit-world as though she were already one of them. In one of these attacks she lay for nine hours, her limbs rigid. From this date, showing the mental aura engendered by the disorder, occurred some strange alterations in her habitual modes of speaking. She never, for instance, spoke of persons as dead, but as having left their shells and gone away. Tested as to the phenomenon of prevision, in one of these trances she would predict to the hour and minute when the next would supervene, and her predictions were, without exception, verified.

There were, it should be added, certain cerebral exponents accompanying these attacks. They were invariably heralded by a buzzing in the head, and followed by soreness at the base of the brain, indicating lesion of the medullary centres. They were accompanied, also, by the phenomenon of cerebral lucidity, she describing her brain as lighted up, and herself as seeing with the top of her head.

Case XVI.—The Rev. William Tennant, of New Jersey, subject from boyhood to nervous attacks, while conversing with his brother on the state of his soul, suddenly fell down in a trance, in which he lay for three days, completely unconscious of what was passing around. He states that it was as if some invisible intelligence took him by the hand and wafted him along, until he came in sight of an exceeding glory, in which swam angelic forms. He heard music that made all earthly music tame in comparison, but, when he wished to join the shining host, his angel *cicerone* gently detained him, and announced to him that he must return to earth. Full of sorrow, he was about remonstrating, when he suddenly found himself in bed in his own house, and saw his brother and the doctor standing near his bed in anxious consultation. His trance did not seem to him to last ten minutes.

Case XVII.—A boy of ten years of age, the son of a washer-woman in New York City, highly intelligent, but subject to fits of absence, and to epileptic convulsions, was observed by a clergyman, who had taken an interest in him, to be in the habit of crossing and recrossing the street without any apparent reason, and to have a kind of terror of coming within the atmosphere of some persons, obviously strangers to him, while taking no pains to avoid others. When the clergyman questioned him as to his reason for avoiding one person rather than another, he invariably replied: "That man is bad; I can see evil spirits flocking about him and filling his mind with wicked thoughts."

One night, two women, well known for benevolence, were called to the death-bed of a consumptive woman—the boy's mother. In the room were the two Sisters of Mercy, the boy, now twelve years of age, and his two sisters. The woman was dying, but still had strength to beckon her son. The two whispered together for a minute, and the conversation ended with the woman saying, "Is that all?" When the fatal moment came, the boy fell down in a fit, and could not be startled out of his lethargy until all was over, when he got up of his own accord, crying, "Mother is happy, and I am satisfied." Taking advantage of his momentary absence from the room, the ladies questioned his sisters as to the meaning of this strange pantomime. "Oh! my brother sees spirits," answered one of them naïvely, "and mother called him to ask what some dark forms were that she saw around the bed. He said they were messengers sent to take her away. Then mother said, 'Is that all?' and died."

CASE XVIII.—Charles Matthews, comedian, subject from boyhood to epileptic attacks. This case illustrates the action of nerve-aura at considerable distances.

Soon after the demise of his first wife, while Mr. Matthews, then comparatively unknown, was playing in London, he was the subject of a singular vision. He had returned from the theatre one evening in a peculiarly restless mood. He went to bed, but was unable to sleep. Ideas and fancies crowded upon him; he turned and turned in bed, but slumber evaded him as it evades the insane in the stage of incubation. He would have rung for a light, and have read for an hour or two—a habit of his before going to sleep, which he had that night neglected—but that it was late, and the house was already silent. In this state, therefore, he lay for an hour or more, until a faint rustle, as of drapery, disturbed the current of his reverie, and, turning his head in the direction whence it came, there stood his wife in her habit as she lived. Smiling sweetly the while, the spectre bent to take his hand, when he started up in terror, and fell to the floor insensible. The fall wakened his landlord, and he was taken up in a fit, from which he did not recover for several days.

Isolated, this commends itself to medical analysis as a simple epileptic attack, with the usual prodromata of restlessness and abnormal nervous excitation. But what complicates it is that an actress, who afterward became his wife and wrote his biography, and who resided in an adjacent street, was at the same instant, as near as could be ascertained, the subject of the same vision, to be taken up in the same manner, insensible. The same unaccountable restlessness had precluded slumber, and culminated at the same moment in a vision of the late Mrs. Mathews, a sudden nervous shock, then insensibility.

A strange case. But it seems evident that the

origin of the fit was with Mr. Mathews, while that of his mistress was a reproduced attack, corresponding in every detail with its original.

CASE XIX.—Let me here, at the risk of egotism, detail briefly a series of psychological phenomena, pertaining principally to my own dream-life, and therefore susceptible of more minute analysis than those of a third person. I will premise that years of study and deprivation had preceded.

In 1858, while a resident of New Germantown, New Jersey, I was acquainted with Mr. Lake, since a Lutheran clergyman, who lived at German Valley, a hamlet lying two leagues to the north. I had never been there. One afternoon, in August, Mr. Lake paid me a visit, and, after dining with me, returned home. That night I dreamed that, while sauntering along the road to German Valley, I came suddenly, at a turn, upon a beautiful vista, that impressed itself on my memory, as dream-vistas often will. Of course, I thought no more of it, except as an addition to my stock of the beautiful; and as Mr. Lake and I started for Hartwick Seminary, Otsego County, New York, a few days after, I never returned the visit. Two years later, while on a vacation visit to New Germantown, business called me to German Valley, and, at a turn of the road, I came full upon the vista of my dream. From that point on, I remembered every landmark, and threaded the way to the village as familiarly as though I had, at some date previous, been in the daily habit of doing so.

In August, 1864, I find myself in New York—a stranger in a strange city. I had been in the city twice or thrice before, *in transitu*, in my driftings to and fro, but was totally unacquainted with it except from geographical description, having to that date known more of the dim dream-cities of Germany—its antique university towns—than of the buzzing metropolis. I had been in New York some days, had exhausted the last dollar of my slender resources, and was in danger of starvation. One sultry evening I lounged up Broadway in the direction of my little room in Bleecker Street, the rent of which had, fortunately, been paid in advance, having eaten nothing for forty-eight hours, but muttering scraps of rhyme as I went. I remember that sunset loiter as though it had been but yesterday. The first gnawings of hunger had worn off; I was faint and flighty, but less uncomfortable than I had been twenty-four hours previous, in that settled exhaustion had succeeded to the stage of acute craving. I knew the end was at hand, and had some dim intention of hastening it: consequently, destroyed every paper and letter in my possession that could possibly identify me. Having done so, I sat and wrote until long after midnight, toiling away at a ballad—"Broadway," I afterward entitled it—that had been running in my brain all the afternoon. On and on I wrote, until I nodded with weariness; but I went to bed at last, and drifted to sleep, conning driblets of rhyme by the way, and keeping up a semi-delirious drone of verses until I finally lost consciousness.

I had a single flash of dream—one only—then slept as one dead until noon the next day.

In my dream I walk down Broadway, cross City Hall Square, and stop at a door with No. 19 over it in gilt numerals. I enter, thread dusty flights of stairs for four stories, and pause at last before a door labeled, "Editorial Rooms," in dingy gilt letters on a black ground. Pushing open the door, I find myself in the midst of a knot of gentlemen, pass through, and tap at the door of an interior room with the knob of my walking-stick. The door opens, and I am face to face with a tall and sad-faced gentleman, of quiet but kindly ways, who asks me to come in. After a conversation of possibly five minutes, consumed in questions on his part and answers on mine, the sad-faced gentleman takes me to an adjoining room and introduces me to a corpulent, falcon-faced gentleman, whom he styles the city-editor, and who, in his turn, presents me to one of the knot in the outer room, with instructions to explain my duties for the evening. This done, I thread my way down-stairs, and as I pass glance at the City-Hall clock. *It is ten minutes past three.* It has passed like a flash—the dream—and I am sound asleep again.

Now, so curiously perverse is human nature that when I started down-town in the afternoon—it must have been two o'clock—it did not occur to me to follow out my dream. I lounged down Broadway listlessly, and, with mind curiously at rest, crossed City-Hall Square instinctively, passed the Hall of Records, and did not even recall the dream until I was at the door of No. 19—when came recognition. I entered, went up-stairs, recognizing even the dusty banisters, and at the remembered landing stopped in front of the door labeled "Editorial Rooms." It was the same. I pushed it open and entered, finding myself in the midst of a group of gentlemen, every one of whom—from rubicund-visaged Dunn to sad-fated Watson—I had met the night before in dream-life. Crossing the room, I tapped at the inner door—one of three—with the top of my walking-stick. The door opened, and there stood the sad-faced man—the late Isaac C. Pray. I was then presented to the falcon-faced city-editor—Mr. John Armstrong. There was no more vagueness about the recognition of either than there would have been had either been my own brother, instead of the perfect stranger he actually was. I was then presented to the subordinate—Mr. J. Edmund Burke. It is a curious fact that I was not at all impressed with these coincidences, but accepted them rather as matters of course than as events partaking of the phenomenal; and as I emerged from the building, with instructions to report at Union Square at seven o'clock, I did not glance at the dial with any intention of verifying my dream to the last circumstance, but merely to ascertain how long I had to rest—for I was weary beyond words—before reporting for further orders. *Nevertheless, it was exactly ten minutes past three.*

I will adduce only one more case of this type, and one of no great importance in one aspect, but of peculiar significance in another. In October, 1872, I was one of the editors of the *Home Journal*. One night, in a flash of dream, the senior editor, Mr. George Perry, called me to his desk for consultation upon a trifling question. As I dreamed it, it was a quarter-past two by the clock just over my left shoulder, as I stood talking with him. The next day, at the hour and minute, that consultation occurred, and verified the dream to the minutest detail. Wholly without premeditation—for the dream had not even occurred to me from the hour I sat down at my desk, between ten and eleven in the morning, until it was abruptly recalled by the remark of Mr. Perry, "Fairfield, I'd like to talk with you a minute"—the exact words with which, as I had dreamed it, the conversation was commenced.

Certain peculiarities distinguishing them from ordinary dreaming have always accompanied these flashes of consciousness. 1. They are invariably instantaneous, preceded by nothing, followed by nothing—sudden islands of dream in a sea of sleep!—and consist, however complex in details, of one swift impression. 2. Apart from myself, I see myself doing this or that as a kind of double, whereas, in ordinary dreaming, there is no double consciousness.

To be more explicit, in ordinary dreaming I am conscious of myself as taking part in this or that transaction, as pursued by ghouls, or taking a walk down Broadway and meeting an Egyptian pyramid at a particular corner; while in these rarer phenomena I, as a spectator, see myself doing a given act, conscious that the doer is a kind of double of mine—conscious of identity also, but still not identical.

In the spring of 1867, after many days of suffering with neuralgia in the right temple, I managed to get detailed from the home-staff for a few weeks, and was sent on a correspondent's commission to Connecticut, which practically enabled me to lounge a few days at the homestead in Stafford. I had left in occupancy of my rooms in town a young man in whom I took a friend's and a student's interest—an example of morbid psychological anatomy, and the victim of attacks of suicidal impulse. I was at home. At a quarter before seven, by the clock in the old east room, as I was pacing to and fro, I was smitten with a sudden spasm of numbness, lasting possibly a second, and succeeded by a rapid flash of vision. I saw the young man with a vial of dark liquid in his hand, in the act of putting it to his mouth. I saw the room, as if a lightning-flash had suddenly lit it up for an instant, and noticed that the sofa had been moved from one corner to another—which was the fact. So possessing was the vision, that I cried, "Stop!" before the absurdity of doing so at that distance occurred to me. Mere fancy, some will say, conjured by worry; but, as exactly as can be ascertained, the young man was, at the instant specified, in the act of putting a vial of laudanum to his lips; and he stated to me afterward that he was deterred from drinking the whole ounce by an uncontrollable force. "It was," said he, "as if some invisible person had taken hold of my hand, and forcibly prevented me from drinking; and, somehow, I didn't dare to try it again after that." Now, curiously enough, my premonition that the young man would kill himself before I got back, which had haunted me during the whole journey thus far, passed away with the shock, the vision, and the consequent shout; and though I was absent from town nearly three weeks longer, and did not once hear from him, I was not in the least worried. I seemed to know, as if by instinct, that the danger was past, and would not again recur; whereas, until then, I had been oppressed as with a spectre.

In June, 1868, having rooms at a Broadway hotel, I was, after some weeks of over-work, prostrated with a kind of nervous fever, and lay for some days in a state bordering upon delirium. My rooms were so distant from the street that, under ordinary circumstances, its scurry was subdued to a continuous roar. As I came to myself I was conscious of hearing with analytic distinctness the feet of persons on the walk, and of an interwoven and inextricable tangle of separate noises caused by stages and carriages. They were not louder than usual, only more distinct. I could tell when a stage stopped and a passenger alighted or got in, and lay and counted by the hour the footsteps of pedestrians, often following one person among the mass for squares, until he turned into a by-street, or faded into distance. Properly speaking, this phenomenon was not due to the excitation of the auditory nerves, though there was unusual acuteness in that direction, but to distinct impulses transmitted by way of the walls of the building. In a word, vibrations of material media, so minute as under ordinary circumstances to be imponderable, were appreciated by the nervous system, and entered into the impressions of consciousness. In addition to this, within a circle of moderate periphery, say twenty feet in diameter, I saw with superhuman distinctness. For example, I saw and knew persons passing in the hall, possibly ten feet from the bed, with the wall between, but could not distinguish them, except as they flitted across the disk of a circle to which my vision was limited. I say *saw*, when I should say that I knew in a manner that was at once vision and audition; yet I did not once pass into the trance-state, though lying for four days just on its border. I may say, therefore, that I personally know that clairvoyance is in the nature of a peripheral nerve-aura of greater or less diameter, this aura entering into intimate molecular relation and contact with surrounding objects; and I am justified, I think, in regarding the nervous phenomena of this attack as entitled to the consideration of facts experimentally demonstrated.

Once more: and the phenomena in this instance may throw some light on the genesis of spirit-poems, like those of Miss Doten and mediums of that class.

In the summer of 1862, having occasion for the services of a dentist, I was subjected to anæsthesia, the agent being sulphuric ether. I recall, as though it had been but yesterday, the strange operation of the drug, and the gradual dying, nerve by nerve, until waves of unconsciousness enveloped the sensory centres, and my eyes were like stones in my head. But an island of consciousness—an irregular tract, of the limits of which I was aware—persisted in the very top of the head, or in the gray cerebral envelope (cortex of the brain). This was accompanied by sensory impressions of a peculiar type. I saw Dr. Clark drop the napkin; I saw him hurriedly going through with the operation. I saw him lay down the forceps when he had completed it; and was conscious through it all that the cortex of the brain was uniquely responsible for these sensory impressions—in a word, that I saw with the top of my head, and through the medium of an external sensory atmosphere.

A strange mental aura, accompanied with nervous perturbation, succeeded, and lasted for some days, during which I was as one in a dream. Its leading exponent consisted in the production of strange and unreal poems, one of which I shall quote, asking the reader to compare it with Poe's ballad of "Ulalume," and to bear in mind that at that time I had never read Poe's ballad:

"The night it was misty and phantasmagorial,
   For the sun had set ashen as lead—
Of his beams shorn, and ashen as lead;
And many a shadow of ancient memorial
   Came up from the tombs of the dead—
Came up on its mission phantasmagorial,
   From the tombs of the legended dead.

"The stars they were shut from my revel—
   From the sight of my wassail and revel,
   In the palace of princes entombed;
For the omens they boded were evil—
   Were omens as men said of evil,
   And of hearts unto ghastliness doomed:
Wherefore, they were shut from my revel,
   In the palace of princes entombed.

"By the light of a triple-winged triad,
   I quaffed from a goblet of gold,
   That was wrought ere the birth of a dryad,
   In the years immemorially old—
That was wrought of red ruby and gold,
Ere the birth of a sylph or a dryad,
   In the years immemorially old—
   In the days of the ghouls immemorially old.

"And I drank of the wine called the living,
   Of the wine that is life to men's souls;
   Of the amethyst extract of souls
I quaffed with no word of misgiving—
With no tremor or word of misgiving—
And I said that as long as earth rolls

I will drink of this liquid of souls;
I was mad with the wine called the living,
And I sang to the princess of ghouls—
To Lilitha, Princess of Ghouls.

"They call the princess of the land of never,
Where worms on beauty dine,
But be thou princess of what land soever,
Come quaff the living wine,
And to thy damnèd ghastliness forever,
Take this mad heart of mine.

"Men say thou dwellest in palaces of shadow,
With hearts ghastlily doomed,
Never to see the asphodel meadow
Of heroes entombed—
That where never a morrow breaks over their sorrow
Thy haunted hearts are entombed.

"But blood-red banners spread their pinions
Over a fabric where shadows dwell,
Drifting, drifting, drifting drearily through pulseless dominions,
To the music of Azrael—
Drifting, drifting, drifting drearily through haunted dominions,
Whose king is Azrael.

" And though at thy grim name the Arab winces,
And his swart lips grow white,
Come quaff the wine of life with me, my princess,
In wild delight,
And it shall thrill thy limbs with life, my princess,
And mad delight.

"Ah, many have fallen unshriven
In the amethyst glory of wine,

And a few stars have wasted from heaven,
Since that ghoul-haunted revel of mine;
But neither unshriven nor shriven
Shall slumber these pulses of mine,
Since by night with the princess of ghouls
I have quaffed of the ghoul-haunted wine—
Ah! neither unshriven nor shriven,
And neither in hell nor in heaven,
Shall they rest from the ghoul-haunted wine."

This is one of several products of the mental aura induced by a single experiment in anæsthesia; and, like the rest, it was written at a sitting, the result of an overbearing impulse, under which I was a mere automaton—rapidly, and in a handwriting so transformed that I doubt whether my most intimate correspondent would have identified it as mine. One fact, however, that disbars the spiritualist interpretation of the phenomenon, is that the handwriting resembled Poe's as little as it did mine. Indeed, although, in my ordinary moods, my hand is very similar to Poe's, that of this manuscript, and of others produced during that period, departs vastly in style from the analytic, continuous, and well-ordered regularity in the formation and grouping of letters common to Poe's manuscript and to my own.

The conclusion, therefore, notwithstanding its resemblance to the ballad of "Ulalume," which I had never read, is that these verses represent simply a transformed nervous impulse, directly and uniquely connected with the morbid intellectual aura engendered by anæsthesia; and in support of this hypothesis I will add that my subsequent experiments with anæsthetics have invariably resulted in similar phenomena.

Without venturing upon disquisition at this juncture, I will merely say in concluding this case that I am of cephalic temperament, and inherit a neurotic tendency from my father; also, that the phenomena have occurred only at periods of exceeding nervous disturbance and of reduced physical condition, and have been invariably accompanied by morbid impulses of more or less intensity: that, in a word, they are purely nervous phenomena.

Case XX.—This case illustrates one aspect of the phenomenon of clairvoyance—that known to exponents of mesmerism as transfer of state, and consisting of the cognition of acts and events present in the memory of a second person. It is, so far as my observations have extended, invariably associated with epileptic neurosis, and occurs spontaneously during the often merely half absence of the larvated fit. Heinrich Zschokke, the Swiss poet and statesman, remarks, in his autobiography, that it has frequently been given to him, on his first interview with a stranger, to see the man's life passing before him like a dream. At first he laid no stress upon these impressions, and regarded them as imaginary and unreal; but subsequent test convinced him of their accuracy as to fact, and he soon learned to rely on them implicitly. He relates, in confirmation of the unerring sagacity of these impressions, that one day at Waldshut, as he was dining with a friend at the hotel, the conversation was turned by a stranger, who sat facing him at the table, upon the peculiarities of the Swiss. The stranger railed at Mesmer and Lavater, until his friend begged him to make some reply, and vindicate the fame of his countrymen.

Zschokke then turned to the stranger. "At that moment," says he, "the man's life passed before me, and I offered to tell him the various events of his past, if he would but confess frankly whether I was correct."

He assented, and Zschokke proceeded with his narrative, event by event, from the student-life of his *vis-à-vis* to his latter career, including, among other details, a liberty he had once taken with the strong box of his principal, and describing the room and the black box on the table, the robbery and the manner of its perpetration. The stranger was astounded, but frankly confessed the exactness and accuracy of the story, cordially shook hands with his tormentor, and departed amid bursts of laughter.

The *rationale* of phenomena of this class will be better comprehended when (if ever) the laws of memory as a nervo-psychic register shall have been more thoroughly elucidated. That the nervous organism registers its succession of states organically cannot be disputed in view of observed facts; but in what manner these nervous states are translated or correlated as states of consciousness, is a problem that is unsolved. The fact that there is an actual correlation accounts, however, for the phenomenon illustrated in this remarkable instance, and removes it from the circle of spiritualist speculation to that of scientific psychology.

Case XXI.—In 1839 Prof. Agassiz submitted himself to a series of experiments conducted by the Rev. C. Hare Townshend, the friend of Dickens, and an acute lecturer on the subject of mesmerism. His description of the first experiment is peculiarly valuable in two respects: 1. As demonstrating that mesmeric slumber resembles the larvated or cerebral fit, in that it is preceded by a nervous shock; 2. As a minute analysis, at the hands of a scientific observer of undoubted veracity, of the psychical phenomena that follow. Agassiz's paper, written the morning after the experiment (February 22, 1839), is entitled "Notes Relatifs au Magnetisme Animal," and has, so far as I am aware, never been published in America.

"Wishing," says the professor, "to form some opinion of mesmerism, I sought an opportunity to experiment upon myself in regard to its phenomena, so as to avoid all doubt as to the actual nature of the sensations. Accordingly, at the instance of M. Desor, I was introduced to Mr. Townshend.

"It was ten o'clock in the evening when, seated facing each other, Mr. Townshend took hold of my hand and began to look at me fixedly. The moment I saw him trying to exert an action on me, I silently addressed the Author of all things, imploring him to enable me to resist and to be conscientious as to the facts. I then fixed my eyes upon the operator. I was in test condition for the experiment, for the hour was one I was in the habit of devoting to study, and I had no disposition to sleep. I was master of myself, able to subdue all emotion and repress all tendency to flightiness of imagination.

" However, at the expiration of at least a quarter of an hour, I felt the sensation of a current through all my limbs, and from that moment my eyes grew heavy. I then saw Mr. Townshend extend his hands before my eyes; then make different circular movements around them, causing them to become still heavier. Then an irresistible heaviness of the lids compelled me to shut them, and gradually I ceased to have the power to keep them open, though I did not the less retain the consciousness of what was going on around me. I heard M. Desor speak and Mr. Townshend answer, and knew what they said. I also heard the questions they asked me, but was incapable of answering, though I tried to speak. When, at last, I succeeded in framing an articulation, I perceived that I was passing out of the state of torpor, which had been rather agreeable than the contrary.

" In this state I heard the cry of ten o'clock; then I heard the clock strike the quarter past. After that I fell into a deeper sleep, although I did not completely lose consciousness. It appeared to me that Mr. Townshend was exerting himself to render me unconscious, and my movements seemed to be under his control, for I wished repeatedly to alter the position of my arms, but could not, nor had the power to will it, although I felt my head carried to the right or left shoulder, and backward and forward, without wishing it, and even in opposition to my wishes. I experienced also a pleasant sensation in giving way to the attraction; then a kind of wonder, when my head fell into Mr. Townshend's hand, which appeared to be the cause of that attraction.

"To his inquiry whether I was well, and how I felt, I was unable to reply, but I smiled—that is, felt my features expand into a smile that I was unable to resist. From that moment I wanted to wake up and was a little restive; yet, when Mr. Townshend asked me if I wished to be awakened, I made a hesitating movement with my shoulders. He then repeated his passes, and I fell into a deeper sleep, though I was still conscious of what was passing around me.

"He then asked me if I would like to become lucid, meanwhile continuing the passes from the face to the arms; and I suddenly experienced an indescribable sensation of delight, rays of dazzling light dancing before my eyes for an instant, then disappearing. I was now inwardly sorry at this state being prolonged, and wanted to wake up, but could not. Still, when Mr. Townshend and M. Desor spoke, I heard them. I also heard the clock strike, and the hour-cry in the street, but did not know what hour was cried. Mr. Townshend then tested me with the usual experiments to ascertain whether I was clairvoyant, but I was unable to distinguish any thing. The clock struck the quarter, and I heard it.

"Mr. Townshend then made some quick transverse movements from the face laterally, which instantly opened my eyes. I got up and said, 'I thank you.' It was a quarter-past eleven o'clock. The operator then told me, and M. Desor repeated it, that the only fact that had satisfied them that I was in mesmeric sleep was the facility with which my head followed the movements of Mr. Townshend's hand, although there was no contact."

CASE XXII.—Florence Cook, of cephalic-vital temperament, lies entranced in an adjoining room, while the phantom form of a lady in luminous robes suddenly appears in the parlor, the phantom bearing a vague resemblance to the medium. Scientific tests have been tried by Mr. Varley, the eminent electrician, and by Prof. Crookes, with the result of demonstrating the non-identity of the medium and the phantom, the latter having had an opportunity of observing Miss Cook lying in trance, while the apparition in white robes was standing by her. During these *séances* Miss Cook lies in deep trance, bordering on catalepsy.

CASE XXIII.—Dr. Henry Sylvester Cornwell, of New London, Conn., of cerebro-vital temperament and inherited consumptive tendency, feels at intervals the contact of spirit-hands; and, united to singular fecundity and strangeness of imagination, analogous to that of Poe, and participating in the same series of morbid sensorial impressions, exhibits an intellectual aura resembling that of the late John Worth Edmonds, but has no sensory cognition of environing intelligences.

I have instanced this case in the nervo-psychic series of phenomena, associated with spiritualism, rather as prefacing the remark that the sensation described by Dr. Cornwell is incident to a state of the nervous system, than as important in itself: a symptom, and a very frequent symptom, in nervous disorders, not a spiritual phenomenon; and a symptom never dissociated, so far as I have observed, from reflex excitability, and always significant of actual nervous disturbances. Inheriting a neurotic tendency, I have personally experienced this sensation at different periods of my life, and have learned to regard it as the invariable precursor of pronounced morbid phenomena—as calling for tonics, not for table-tipping.

Of the thirty-nine cases of inherited neurosis in which I have made particular inquiry as to this symptom, it has been distinctly present in twenty-seven, as one of the prodromata of impending disturbance of a more serious nature. In the instance of Judge Edmonds, for example, this symptom preceded the more exaggerated symptom of spirit-seeing. Not in the nature of an hallucination, because a real sensation resulting from morbid excitability of the peripheral nerves, the phenomenon is like sudden contact, sometimes very soft, sometimes very pronounced, with invisible hands; so like it, indeed, that, wakened out of a reverie by the sensation of a hand on my shoulder, I have often turned instinctively, expecting to find some person standing behind me. In my own case this symptom has generally coexisted with another that I can only describe as the hearing of inner voices.

CASE XXIV.—Dr. C. S. Sprague, of Stafford, Connecticut, whose father was a practising physician for many years previous to his death, relates that his first case in the town where he now practises, was a case of typhoid fever. His father, it should be premised, died when he was a mere lad. He was exceedingly anxious concerning the case, as his success in his profession was somewhat dependent on it, and returned from his visit in a state of worry and nervousness that no distraction of attention served to dissipate. He fell asleep that night, cogitating on the *indicia* of the case, and the best method of correcting them, and passed, with scarcely a break in consciousness, from cogitation and worry to a dream, in which his father appeared standing by the bed, and distinctly explained to him that the symptoms indicated certain remedies. The doctor adopted the suggestions of the spirit, and the patient recovered. Dr. Sprague deposes that he had never had any conversation with his father, an homœopathic physician, concerning the *indicia* of typhoid fever, and that his dream could not have sprung from any unconscious reminiscence of his father's practice. In explanation of this phenomenon, as in the similar case quoted by Mr. Macnish, the physiologist is irresistibly impelled to adopt the hypothesis of the heredity of special nervous impressions, or, in better terms, to extend the process of hereditary transmission so as to cover, not only the general habits and nervous idiosyncrasies of an ancestor, but the particular impressions recorded in his nervous organism as subjects of conscious recollection; so that, under circumstances of unusual nervous perturbation, one may recollect, if the word may be permitted, ideas and events originally impressed upon the recollection of his father or grandfather, but with which he is totally unacquainted by verbal or written record; and thus, to put the ascertained facts in the form of a proposition, any impression recorded in the nervous organization of an ancestor is potential in the nervous organization of his descendants. I have been able to investigate thoroughly, from this aspect of the subject, but very few cases of monomania, and shall prosecute the examination at further length hereafter; but the few I have been able to bring under the microscope (if that metaphor be permissible) have served to convince me that medical men must, in some cases at least, seek for the etiology of the special forms that monomania takes, in the heredity of special nervous impressions, which, in the ancestor, may not have risen to the intensity of mania. If, again, as must be presumed in this instance, the vision incident to the actualization of the impression, present to the conscious recollection of the father, but potential only in the organism of the son, was the sequel of its heredity, a new and singular aspect of the law of association, as it pertains to psychological phenomena, presents itself to the view of the psychologist. The case adduced by Mr. Macnish and that of Dr. Sprague are coincident in respect to the vision; and, with other cases, which Dr. Gieser, a plodding German, has collected and verified, but from which he has neglected—being an exponent of the theories of animal magnetism—to draw any valuable conclusions, seem to me to indicate that the law of association is more deeply grounded in nervous organization, and constitutes a more important element in our psychical experiences than has been generally supposed, even by the most devout disciples of Mr. James Mill. It may, from this aspect, be held responsible for one class of the visions occurring in trance and clairvoyance; while, considered as a source of the strange intelligence associated with these nervous states, it is certainly of great importance. Dr. Sprague is of pronounced nervous temperament.

CASE XXV.—J. R. Brown, of Iowa, twenty-one years of age, and of cerebro-vital temperament. His clairvoyance resembles that of Miss L—— in its initial stages. Finds and describes articles by the process generally turned thought-reading. His trances are preceded by slight nervous shocks, and he exhibits symptoms of exceeding physical exhaustion when his *séances* have been at all prolonged, or have called for more than ordinary feats.

CASE XXVI.—A well-known lawyer, of large practice in the State of Connecticut, gives several instances in which he has been impressed of coming events in dreams. On one occasion he dreamed that his nephew, a little boy of four years old, had fallen into a well and been drowned. A few days later he was called to attend the funeral of that nephew, whose death had taken place in the exact manner foreshadowed. On another occasion, he dreamed that his brother, then living in New Jersey, and in good health for aught he knew to the contrary, came in at the east door of the old house where his boyhood was passed, haggard and wan with illness, and that he looked up at the clock as his brother entered, and noticed that it was just four in the afternoon. The dream worried him a little the next morning, but he had quite forgotten it, and was sitting in the east room of the old house, poring over a legal treatise, when a feeble step was heard in the space that led from the open wood-house to the east door; then the door opened, and his brother walked wearily in. It was exactly four o'clock; and the strangest part of it all was, that this brother, who had been absent for some months, was dressed exactly as he had seemed to be in the dream of the previous night, and in a suit he had procured after leaving home.

I conclude this series, which might be extended into a volume, with this case; merely observing that the theory of accidental coincidences, so often called in by scientific men for their explanation, breaks down under practical tests, and that the brain-wave hypothesis, although undoubtedly competent to the explanation of the more ordinary phenomena here instanced, has, in addition to the fact that it is unverifiable—an invented hypothesis, not one flowing directly from the nature of the facts to be elucidated, but a mere extension of the wave-theory of light —no application to the presentiment and prevision that so frequently occur in these nervous states, and must therefore be dismissed to the limbo of clever but inadequate attempts to give coherence and uniformity to a troublesome series of facts, without being at the pains to investigate them thoroughly. They are facts that call for careful analysis of all the conditions under which they occur, not for hasty generalization.

IV.

PHYSIOLOGY OF THE NERVO-PSYCHIC SERIES.

I HAVE purposely permitted the preceding memoranda of cases to take a large range, and to exceed the limits apparently prescribed by the subject, by way of illustrating the psychic phenomena associated with spiritualism in all the protean aspects in which they are or may be exhibited.

In the majority of these instances I have been able to verify the existence of an hereditary predisposition. So, also, in many cases the psychic phenomena of which are not so pronounced as to be worthy of particular description. Mrs. Isabella B. Hooker, of Hartford, Connecticut, for example, inherits nervous malady from her father. So with the daughter of the late Judge Edmonds—a medium of considerable repute, whose habit of trance-speaking, in languages unknown to her through the ordinary process of study, has been examined *en passant*, and who presents, physically, one of the most pronounced examples I have ever glanced at, of the congeries of symptoms associated with active neurosis of this type. Again, in the case of Robert Dale Owen—by far the most intellectual literary exponent of spiritualism in America—hereditary predisposition plays an important part, as is evident from keen scrutiny of the career and personal history of the elder Owen.

It frequently happens that an inherited neurotic tendency exhibits itself in a very different form in different members of the same family. In the instance of Mrs. Hooker, for example, occur the ordinary physical exponents of inherited nervous disorder, conjoined to a tendency to vagary and eccentricity, that borders upon aberration of mind; while in her sister, Mrs. Stowe, and in other members of the family, so far as I am able to ascertain, the predisposition expends itself in a well-marked and peculiar mental aura, with psychical and emotional traits *sui generis*. In like manner, in Miss Lamb, the sister of the humorist, the hereditary predisposition manifested itself in periodical attacks of an epileptic nature, while in her gifted brother (Charles Lamb) it was mainly present as an intellectual bias, and contributed its rarest gems to the literature of humor. Indeed, as those eminent alienists, Morel, Moreau de Tours, Dr. Maudsley, and Dr. Anstie, have long since demonstrated, not only are the various neuroses constantly convertible, but hereditary neurosis frequently exhibits itself as an intellectual aura, without pronounced nervous disturbance, though generally coexistent with a moodiness having more or less tendency to periodicity.[1] This observation has been verified so often that it is unnecessary to adduce instances.

In this aspect of the subject, hereditary neurosis of the dormant variety must be regarded as the cause of many of the most wonderful creations in literature and art.

Minute analysis of the biography of Poe discloses the fact that his most remarkable tales and poems exhibit a periodicity of imaginative production: he himself says that poetry with him was a passion, not a profession. So it was with Coleridge, and so it was with that wonderful boy whose literary forgeries so long baffled criticism, and who called his cantos fit the first, fit the second, and so on—all

[1] The three sisters of Gilbert Stuart, the celebrated portrait-painter, whose fitful moroseness was the puzzle of his friends, were all early subject to epileptic paroxysms. One of them, an artist herself of singular felicity in portraits, died a raving maniac at Butler Hospital. Another was for years a confirmed maniac; the third had quiet intervals. A singular fatality, as the records of Butler Hospital intimate, followed the Allston family, of whom the famous Washington Allston is the most generally remembered. The father of Raphael d'Urbino was, it is estimated by Passavant, subject to paroxysms of clairvoyance and presentiment; and if, in general, the ancestors of men and women of strange powers of imagination were to be subject to vigilant investigation, it would, no doubt, clearly appear that the etiology of certain singular aspects of this faculty, as illustrated in the biography of those who have startled the world by strange creations in poetry and the kindred arts, is to be sought in a kind of larvated type of hereditary neurosis. Dr. Maudsley, in the position he assumes on this question, is supported by the closest scrutiny of the facts.

fits—finally a suicidal fit that ended him. Dr. Johnson was the son of an epileptic. Turner's sunsets, with their sun-shot purples and semi-glooms, are the products of a strange man; and William Blake, the strangest of English painters, painted like a man in trance. Wellington's epilepsy disappeared on the field, his accumulated nervous force finding a conductor active enough to dissipate it as fast as it was generated.

The career of Robespierre, with his sunken temples, and face eternally jerking, is to be regarded, from the scientific stand-point, as the exponent of hereditary nervous disorder, intensified by deprivation at first, and afterward by the circumstances of the Revolution in France. Mohammed's revelations represent a series of epileptic trances; Swedenborg's confess the same etiology; and, generally speaking, as Dr. Maudsley acutely observes, there is no doubt that mankind is indebted for not a little of its originality, and for certain special forms of intellectual activity, to individuals who have sprung from families in which the neurotic tendency is hereditary. The wonderful mastery of morbid psychology exhibited by writers like Scott, Dickens, Poe, Hawthorne, Heyne and Freytag, Baudelaire and Victor Hugo—and of morbid impulse in its various aspects—thus presents itself as a kind of larvated form of nervous perversion, liable always to transformation into the acute, and often coexisting with it.

In America—at least in the New England States and in New York, to which my observations have been principally limited—I have no hesitation in saying that alcohol has played a prominent part in the production of nervous degeneracy; and, with Dr. Anstie, I am inclined to think that of all depressing agencies it has the most decided tendency to impress the nervous centres of a progenitor with a neurotic type that will necessarily be transmitted to his descendants. That it often produces epilepsy within a single generation, is a demonstrable fact, though alcoholic epilepsy is not yet known to the medical text-books. Unscientific preparation and insufficiency of food, conjoined to hard work on the part of the women, and harder work on the part of the men, have also been exceedingly active causes, particularly in the New England States, in perverting the nervous organization; and though Niemeyer's estimate, applicable to Germany, that the ratio of epileptics to general population is one to one hundred, is probably in excess of the facts in this country, it is nevertheless true that obscure epilepsy is alarmingly common.

Omitting *grand mal*, or falling-sickness, from the discussion, I shall limit myself to the three types of *petit mal*—fits of absence or of intellectual eclipse, lasting generally but a few seconds, with pallor and stupefaction as its symptoms; vertiginous epilepsy, with its more or less prolonged suspension and its partial convulsions of the face; cerebral or larvated epilepsy, with its absence of contemporaneous convulsions—and to that important variety known as the nocturnal paroxysm.

Calmeil, who was the first to demonstrate the epileptic nature of the fit of absence, regards it as an averted attack of vertigo; while Herpin observes that it is always possible to detect some slight partial shock in every case of absence, and some slight partial convulsions. These attacks, says Herpin, are never ushered in by complete unconsciousness, nor by the wild initial cry; and though the *never* of that eminent authority states the case too forcibly, it is nevertheless true that the nervous shock is not always accompanied by loss of consciousness. The nocturnal paroxysm often occurs unsuspected even by the victim, or is registered simply as nightmare, and frequently eludes the observation of vigilant physicians.

How difficult it is to detect epilepsy in these obscure forms, and to what extent it contributes in determining the direction of the intellectual activity, are illustrated daily in medical psychology. I was on somewhat intimate terms with Mansfield Tracy Walworth for several years previous to his death, and meanwhile engaged in investigating, from life, morbid psychology in its various forms; but it was not until I had known him two years that I began to suspect that the somewhat singular traits, psychical and intellectual, illustrated in his novels, had their origin in the epileptic malady; although the existences of peculiar nervous impulses—one of them his habit of carrying his hand to his breast impulsively in moments of animation—had not escaped me. One day, within a few months of his tragic death, Mr. Walworth and myself were standing on the corner at the Fifth Avenue Hotel, engaged in conversation, when I observed for the moment a peculiar propensity to repeat my remarks before replying, and also to repeat his own final phrases. His eyes were faded, he was pale, and talked like a man in a dream; but recovered suddenly, and was himself again. Indeed, but for the phenomenon of repetition, which is pretty constant in that class of cases, I should not have suspected that the brief fit of absent-mindedness I had just observed was of epileptic nature. Subsequent observation confirmed the impression, however, and furnished the clew to the peculiar psychical and imaginative traits exemplified in his life and literature.

Still more likely to escape the attention even of the average medical observer is the obscure type known as nocturnal epilepsy, and yet no type more rapidly degenerates the nerve-centres alike in structure and function. The extent to which it prevails is indicated by the fact that it is seldom absent in cases of periodical aberration of mind. "I would take pains to affirm," says Dumesnil, "that there is now no patient at the institution under my direction whose insanity is not associated with slight nocturnal attacks, which up to the present have escaped our attention." Trousseau justly remarks that all nocturnal accidents should suggest epilepsy; and my own observations have led me to the conclusion that habitual attacks of nightmare and somnambulism are generally exponents of epileptic neurosis, and are often subject to the periodicity associated with the disorder. This was, no doubt, true in the instance of Mary Carrick; and in another less dramatic instance that recently came under my notice, phenomena of the same specific type, though less pronounced in rappings and other dynamic manifestations, were, upon minute observation, demonstrated to coexist with nocturnal fits, accompanied with stertorous breathing and scarcely perceptible convulsions. In two other instances of settled somnambulism, careful observation has enabled me to detect the periodicity, and, what is more important, the precursory symptom of a slight nervous shock.

I have dwelt thus minutely upon these points, by way of indicating two things: 1. That the popular conception of epilepsy, based principally upon its convulsions, is a very unscientific one, and is incompatible with any just idea of the extent to which it is prevalent; 2. That the whole series of morbid phenomena instanced as nervo-psychic naturally group themselves about the epileptic neurosis under its various transformations, and are always preceded by nervous shocks of greater or less intensity. Also, by way of preface to the discussion of another and more relevant point.

While it is true that occasional epileptic attacks, particularly in women, have a central origin, yet physiological experiments have demonstrated the general truth of Marshall Hall's conclusion that epileptic paroxysms, like all reflex movements, are always traceable to peripheral incitations. Upon this hint Dr. Brown-Séquard acted in that series of experiments that enabled him to disclose the existence of the unfelt aura in epileptic paroxysms, and to demonstrate the fact that irritation of the peripheral nerves arrests and prevents the attack in artificial epilepsy. Acting upon the same principle, Herzen and Lewison have been able to demonstrate that so long as irritation of the peripheral nerves is continued, no reflex excitability of the spinal cord can occur. In a similar manner, in the only three instances in which I have been able to induce mediums to submit to the experiment, I have been able to arrest the supervention of the trance by peripheral irritation, thus demonstrating that, in these three instances at least, the phenomena were due to reflex excitability. In this manner, or upon this principle, M. Foissac was able, in the case of Pierre Cazot, to transform the convulsions of *grand mal* into the trance or larvated type of the attack.

Nor will this hypothesis of the epileptic origin of these phenomena seem exceptional in the light of the facts, when it is considered that Niemeyer is proximately correct in stating the ratio of epileptic persons to the general population to be as one to one hundred: ample verge here for spiritual mediums by the score: and that, as the eminent Calmeil was the first to prove, those fits of absence that Mr. Macnish so cleverly discusses in his paper on abstraction, particularly as respects the cases of Hogarth, Dr. Robert Hamilton, the Rev. Dr. Harvest, and Prof. Warton, are really of epileptic nature and but semi-averted paroxysms—always ushered in, as Herpin observes, by scarcely perceptible shocks, but not attended with complete unconsciousness nor with the wild initial cry that, once heard, can never be forgotten. In this aspect of the malady lies the solution of the dramatic case of M. Cazotte, and that of the equally dramatic case of Captain Densmore.

Theoretically and observationally, therefore, it seems to me evident that the psychical phenomena associated with spiritualism are the exponents of nervous lesion; also, that this lesion belongs to the epileptic type, to which as a centre is tethered a startling circle of weird sensorial impressions, and of apparently preternatural states of consciousness, involving in its nocturnal aspects premonitory dreams, and in its diurnal the elements of presentiment and prevision. And the strangest part of it all is, that our lives so often verify these dreams and premonitions as to disbar their relegation to the category of fortuitous coincidences. It is demonstrable, however, that, so far from supporting the hypothesis of spiritual intervention, these phenomena lie strictly within the circle of nervous and cerebral disturbance; that, therefore, their existence in any given case is in no way indicative of higher psychical organization, as the exponents of spiritualism presume. On the other hand, they are constantly convertible with the more ordinary phenomena of epilepsy, constantly preceded by slight nervous shocks, and only occur as the exponents of nervous perversion, either hereditary or acquired.

Furthermore: in studying the foregoing cases, the reader will observe that clairvoyance is the type of the psychical group. In the course of this inquiry I have visited eleven different clairvoyant physicians and mediums, with a view to test the question whether the nervous shock preceded the psychical phenomenon. In four of these cases, the shock was so slight as to produce a barely perceptible tremor; in six, visible jerkings of the arm announced the supervention of the state; in one, in which I was unable to detect any external indications, the medium confessed that a kind of nervous thrill and shudder invariably foreran the clairvoyant condition.

I shall have to except from this generalization, however, cases of vision, like that of Mr. Mathews, in which, as the product of a sort of intellectual aura, preceding, as Falret well observes, the supervention of the convulsions, the sensory impression heralds the attack or shock. One gentleman, subject to attacks of *grand mal*, always sees just as the fit supervenes, but only with the left eye, a hideous black-and-red human figure, that gradually magnifies as it moves toward him. Others see flames, fiery circles, red or purple objects; or hear the sound of far-off bells, or voices repeating the same word over and over; but by far the most frequent sensorial impression incident to this stage, and preceding the shock, is the ghost or phantom. Again, it not seldom happens that no convulsions occur, and then the fit is wholly represented by the mental aura and its consequent sensory impressions, without perceptible nervous tremor. Lasting a few minutes, it is ushered in, not by unconsciousness, but by a strange sensation of passing suddenly from one world to another. This type—the fit of absence in its subtilest form—pretty accurately describes the case of Judge Edmonds, and merits perhaps the distinctive appellation of intellectual epilepsy. These impressions, variable as they are in individuals, reproduce themselves from fit to fit with singular uniformity; yet that they in no way imply lesion of the optic nerves is exemplified in the case of the gentleman who saw the hideous black-and-red figure with the left eye, the vision of the right eye continuing normal, although the ophthalmoscope was incompetent to detect the slightest difference between the left optic nerve and its fellow : so that it is evident that in these instances the impression is due to causes of cerebral origin, and that Falret is correct in denominating the aura, whence these impressions spring, an intellectual aura.

It requires an exceedingly acute eye, habituated to careful observation, to detect and finally trace to their source the symptoms indicative of this obscure form of the disorder. I have in my mind's eye, at this moment, a lady of intensely cerebral organization, with whom I was intimately acquainted for many months, and who in certain peculiar moods was a rampant spiritualist, while ordinarily skeptical on the subject—intimately acquainted for many months, before I detected the existence of a distinct periodicity in these moods, and on closer observation was able to refer them to their cause. Naturally of keen and penetrative intellect, though imaginative even to the verge of mysticism, in her more normal moments her acute insight rebelled against the doctrines of spiritualism, while in these attacks, with the morbid sensorial visions incident to them, mere denial of its tenets, however gently and courteously expressed, was productive of savage irritation; and thus she lived on in perpetual struggle between morbid spiritual day-dreams and higher and saner views of spiritual life.

The conclusion is, then, that this form of spirit-seeing, as illustrated in the case of Judge Edmonds, is a true intellectual epilepsy, with paroxysms of varying duration, but seldom lasting more than a few minutes, though of frequent occurrence in the settled stages of the disorder.

The extremer form of trance, as it occurs in catalepsy, and often in epileptic attacks, now calls for explanation.

PHYSIOLOGY OF THE NERVO-PSYCHIC SERIES.

Taking into consideration the fact that true insanity is the exponent of a morbid condition of the gray matter of the brain, and the coincident fact that the cortex of the brain, or gray cerebral envelope, is the seat of consciousness, the physiology of this phenomenon is very apparent, strange as its psychic impressions often are. If the reader will trouble himself to follow the details of a dissection, he will observe that the medulla oblongata (or upward continuation of the spinal marrow) represents three pairs of bodies, united in a bulb, and resting in a fossa of bone. Of these, the two pyramidal bodies continue the two frontal threads of the spinal cord, and the two restiform bodies the two posterior threads. The two olivary bodies, consisting of gray matter thinly enveloped in white fibres, continue the gray matter of the spinal cord, and lie interior and partly lateral. Innumerable white fibres, springing from the restiform bodies and passing through masses of gray matter, curve backward, and expand into the two lobes of the cerebellum; while innumerable pyramidal and olivary fibres, with perhaps a few restiform, curving forward and passing through the gray masses, traverse the great ganglia, and finally expand into the two hemispheres and six lobes of the cerebrum.

According to Tiedemann, when these fibres emerge from the ganglia, they form a thin membranous fabric, which thickens as crescence of the organism proceeds, and is at last doubled upon itself fold upon fold, thus forming the convolutions, which vary somewhat in number in the heads of different individuals, and in disorders of the hydrocephalic type, where the cranium is considerably enlarged, are occasionally absent altogether. Indeed, it is not very difficult to unravel the hemispheres of a recently-formed brain, and expand them into membranes. Thus the sexifold spinal stem blossoms into the complex structure of a human brain.[1]

This cortical covering of the brain, consisting of cincritious and vesicular matter, is the seat of consciousness, and at various centres in it appear to originate those impulses of conscious volition that

[1] When I describe the gray neurine of the spinal cord (or its continuation in the olivary bodies) as expanding into the cortex, or lamina forming the external envelope of the brain, I accept a presumption of numerous cerebral anatomists, but one that I have never been able to verify in actual dissection. On the other hand, though the gray matter of the column can be traced in continuous tracts to the corpora striata and the optic thalami, dissection offers no evidence, of a satisfactory kind, that it is structurally responsible for the cortex; and, strictly speaking, the peripheral neurine of the cerebrum and cerebellum must be regarded as structurally distinct from the gray central matter of the spinal system, which is susceptible of receiving impressions (without consciousness) and of reflex action of its own, apart from volition—in a word, is possessed of independent excito-motor properties. The nervous system of the unconscious life is thus completely separable from the laminated structure concerned in the phenomenon of consciousness, which may be hypothetically dissected from it, leaving intact, though unconscious in its operations, the whole sensory and motor organism. The force of this fact will appear by-and-by, when the unconscious volition concerned in a certain class of so-called spiritual phenomena comes under discussion.

constitute, in their varied relations to life, aptitudes and faculties. The great vital centres are the medullary and spinal; the cerebellum is concerned in general muscular coördination; the cerebrum, in cerebration, and in voluntary movements particularly pertaining to intellectual and emotional expression. Electrical excitation of the brain and spinal cord, at the hands of Prof. Ferrier, has demonstrated several points of value in morbid psychology: 1. That the anterior lobes of the brain are the principal centres of voluntary motion and of the active external manifestation of intelligence; 2. That the individual convolutions have the functions of distinct centres; 3. That the action of the hemispheres is generally crossed, though certain movements of the mouth and tongue and neck are bilaterally coördinated; 4. That certain portions of the brain give no muscular response to the current, and are probably appropriated to sensory phenomena and cognition. These unresponsive portions seem to be situated centrally and coronally.[1]

[1] The intimacy of coördination that exists between the brain and the purely automatic physical functions is illustrated by many curious facts. If, for example, the pons Varolii, or medium of communication between the two lobes of the cerebellum, be punctured with a sharp instrument, congestion of the lungs ensues. If, again, the floor of the fourth ventricle of the brain be punctured in the same manner, the kidneys secrete copiously of glucose, a common symptom in diabetes, and in the diabetes that accompanies nocturnal epilepsy. Illustrations of this special class might be quoted to the extent of pages; but the result would be merely to establish that which physiological studies have rendered a non-debatable proposi-

It is very evident, from these facts, that in the profounder order of trance, and in so-called cerebral lucidity, is implied a persistent reflex excitability of the gray sensory matter of the brain, during partial suspension of the medullary (vital) and motor centres; and this view is supported by the fact that trance

tion, namely, that to disturb the function of the brain, or that of any special nerve-centre, is to disturb the whole animal economy. If one point, upon which physiologists have thus far dwelt very sparingly, but which is, nevertheless, fundamental to thorough physiological investigation, is ever placed in its proper attitude by some master, like Dr. Carpenter, the importance of studying organism synthetically, as well as analytically, will be exhibited more clearly than it is in ordinary text-books, or even in special treatises. Let it be considered, as a starting-point, that all tissues, nervous, muscular, osseous, etc., are but transformations of a single primordial tissue as all types of organism have their origin in one primordial form, and the value of what may be styled synthetic physiology is lucidly manifest. From this aspect of the subject, the importance of medical education to the professional physiologist needs only to be pointed out to be appreciated; for it is only by observing the congeries of results, that flow from the disturbance of particular functions, that these mutual relations of physical and psychical phenomena can be fully apprehended. So far as scientific investigation can penetrate, molecular force is the structural force and the study of molecular physics is the study of physics from the stand-point of structure. It will be long, probably, before scientists will be able to trace out, link by link, the vast series of transformations of tissue that enters into the complex structure of the human body; but that the series will finally be traced out no careful journalist of scientific progress can reasonably doubt. Meanwhile, in order to appreciate the intimacy of relation that brain or nerve bears to muscle or bone, let it be remembered that all ultimately merge themselves in a mother-tissue, of which they are successive differentiations, and participate in the same molecular properties.

develops heat in the coronal region of the cranium, and is generally followed by soreness at the back of the neck. This phenomenon involves, therefore, the supposition of lesion of the gray cognitive tract, and, when, through successive stages of nervous degeneration, fostered by morbid vanity, and partly by the morbid impulses it engenders, this sanctum of mind is attacked, the poor broken medium drifts rapidly in the direction of dementia; still exulting, perhaps, in occasional glimpses of his lost lucidness, but generally tormented with the spectre of a life squandered in those sensory dreams in which the literature of spiritualism is so abundant.

The prevision occasionally involved in these morbid states of consciousness is the only element in them that seems to participate in the superhuman. To attempt explanation of this phenomenon, so familiar to medical psychologists, would be to dip deeper into speculative problems than limits at this stage permit. That which more especially differences man from the lower animals is imagination, employing the term to represent the cognitive and creative, the higher emotional energy of the soul. The true artist, like the true poet, is prophetic, and discerns the beautiful that comes by-and-by in the imperfect beautiful that is. Our undeveloped lives are greater than our lives developed. Our real man protests from the cradle to the grave against the littleness of the actual man; and, though a magnificent *physique* is a splendid promoter of skepticism, this our souls within themselves know: that our true real comes not by way of trances, but by way of honest endeavor for the good. The beginning of spiritual revelation is action. Our beautiful is by toil, not by trance. Compassed about by the four baffling and terrible silences of whence and what, and why and whither, as our lives are, it is impossible to refuse a kind of sympathy to those who importune matter and mind for some answers to the riddle; but it is scarcely necessary to accept the answers of the oracle. Nor is it so essential to our spiritual culture that these silences should speak as to justify our acceptance of morbid nervous phenomena as revelations of the supersensible. Our lives are not long enough to juggle with our problems at *séances*, and, were they, our natures are so constituted that insincerity is akin to death.

Yet I ought not, perhaps, so far as consistent with brevity, to shirk the task of explaining, or of offering, aside from their etiology, some rational solution, in more particular terms, of the phenomena of presentiment and premonitory dreams, which, as a curious fact, and a pretty constant one, seldom occur in cases where the vision of spirits is a dominant symptom, and constitute a group by themselves. In their bearing on psychological science, they may be regarded as furnishing inductive proof of Kant's doctrine of the ideality of time and space, absurd as it seems to the inductive thinker who has never been at the pains to collect and verify the facts. The hypothesis of coincidence, so generally insisted upon as responsible for the verification of dreams of this class, breaks down under practical tests, such as were instituted in the cases of Emma L—— and Pierre Cazot, and have been instituted at large by Dr. Gieser. An unerring prevision certainly accompanies morbid nervous function in some cases, generally as an isolated exponent, dissociated from the ordinary psychical phenomena upon which the doctrines of spiritualism rest. In all the cases of prevision in dreams that I have been able to collect, as a constant law, the future presents itself as present to the dreamer, and as the vision of something actually taking place. No consciousness of time appears to be involved, and Dr. Gieser, in his curious museum of instances, mentions no exception to this rule. It is a notable fact, also, that in settled insanity, where the cortex of the brain (or lamina of consciousness) is affected, the idea of time is quite invariably absent. I knew and studied, some years since, the case of an old man who had been insane since he was twenty-one years of age, though at intervals he seemed lucid, but to the day of his death he was only twenty-one. Is there not, then, in view of these facts of morbid function of this special tract, a temptation to agree with Kant and Schopenhauer, and to regard time as a form of consciousness—as that law of normal function by virtue of which the future seems to have no existence as a form of being, except as potential in the present? And, if this be so, then our lives are all embedded in a being that knows no time and no space, and answers the ancient definition of eternity: "*Æternitas non est temporis fine successio, sed nunc stans.*" It should be noted, also, as the constant exponent of clairvoyance, that the distant presents itself as visible and actually present to the inner sight, or, if the term may be permitted, to the cerebral vision. This phenomenon of vision is, let me add, invariably associated with the superficial lamina of gray nervous tissue enveloping the cerebral ganglia, as a congeries of motor and sensory centres. Now, is not the absence of time and space as forms of consciousness in the deeper types of trance, and the partial absence of the latter in its less pronounced types, a fact of great value, not only as indicative of the main source of the intelligence accompanying these states, but in its bearing on scientific psychology, particularly as regards the question suggested by Spinoza ("Cogitata Metaphysica," C. 4), and exhaustively discussed by Kant—with what result has been intimated? For it shows that the permanence of time and space, as forms of consciousness, is uniquely dependent on integrity of cerebral function, and that they are specially absent in instances of morbid function of the cortex as an almost invariable rule; the future presenting itself as existing in the form of present fact, and the distant as a subject of vision. Strange as these laws of morbid psychical phenomena may seem to those who have not given particular attention to the subject, they are nevertheless stated as the results of observations careful and extensive enough to establish them as strict inductions of science. My own view of the case is, that, in molecular disturbances of the nervous system, its peculiar activities become *en rapport* with molecular forces operating externally, accepting and correlating as intelligence vibrations not cognizable at all under ordinary circumstances. It must be remembered, in support of this view, that molecular force is the parent of all forces concerned in natural phenomena, and the source of all organic transformations—the final link between secondary forces and the great First Cause of things. And if time and space are only forms of consciousness, then cause and effect are only forms of consciousness.

If it is now clear that the etiology of this series of phenomena is to be sought in a true nervous lesion, a more striking, though really less important, series demands attention.

V.

NERVE-ATMOSPHERE AND ITS AGENCY IN NERVO-MOLECULAR PHYSICS.

Before entering upon the nervo-dynamic series, it is proper to direct the reader's attention to certain problems in molecular physics, or to certain facts, rather, which lie within the horizon of this investigation, and are essential to a just estimate of its scientific relations. The term *aura* has thus far been employed in its general definition; what that is the reader will gather from its derivation, and from its classical usage, as designating, a nymph of the air, or from its mediæval, to designate the halo of light about the heads and faces of saints.

The series of experiments by a German *savant*, now nearly forgotten, that resulted in the discovery of odic force (*od*), not only illustrate the nature and operations of this element, but also indicate its relation to the nervo-dynamic phenomena associated with spiritualism. These experiments were conducted principally with persons subject to attacks of catalepsy, by the agency of whose thrice-acute nerves it was first ascertained that from the poles of an open magnet were constantly shot two luminous tongues of flame, visible to persons of exceedingly sensitive nervous organization. The luminous tufts emitted from the poles of a large magnet, capable of lifting ninety pounds, were described as somewhat less than a foot in length, and iridescent and flickering. To test whether these phenomena were real, the experimenter prepared a very sensitive plate in the same manner as for the camera of a photographer, and placed it in a box impervious to light, facing the poles of a large open magnet. On the third day the plate was removed and subjected to the action of mercurial vapor. It had been distinctly affected, as by light; while a similar plate, prepared in the same manner, under conditions exactly the same, less the magnet, was totally unaffected at the expiration of the same period—to be exact, sixty-four hours.

The operator now extended his experiments, and ascertained that the points of crystals emitted flames visible to cataleptics, and described by them as resembling tulip-blossoms. On the other hand, amorphous bodies, as was demonstrated by many experiments, presented no similar optical phenomena.

But the more important aspect of the series was this: that magnets and crystals, in common with amorphous bodies, and indeed all substances, emitted a subtile aura, capable of acting on the nerves of a cataleptic at considerable distances, so as to produce spasms, and susceptible of transmission through conducting media. Thus, when a large magnet was placed six paces from the feet of an invalid lady, and the arm removed, she fell into tetanic convulsions, and became unconscious. When, again, the arm was replaced, she recovered consciousness. Another lady, also cataleptic, instantly detected the proximity of an open magnet that had been secretly introduced into an adjacent room. It was, in like manner, ascertained that certain bodies powerfully attracted the hands of cataleptics, even in the unconsciousness of the fit; and that certain other bodies were, under similar circumstances, hurled violently from the hand, that member remaining, after the act, firmly fixed in its new position. The bearing of these facts upon the genesis of phantom phenomena will appear by-and-by.

By frequent repetition of these experiments some of the laws of this new activity of bodies were ascertained, and a real contribution to progress in this direction was made, though one that has been prolific of speculative, and barren of practical results. This one point, however, is pertinent to nervous physiology, namely, that certain bodies, even at a considerable distance, may act powerfully as peripheral incitations in nervous disorders of the epileptic type, and that their specific influences are susceptible of transmission for several hundred feet, and of affecting the nerves at that distance. The intimate reciprocal relation that exists between the nervous system and the molecular constitutions of environing bodies

—a relation impalpable to the senses, but not the less real—could scarcely be better illustrated than by this series. Our lives are environed with molecular influences, that enter into our deepest intuitions of the constitution of matter, and assist, unconsciously to ourselves, in determining our profoundest philosophical conceptions and our subtlest psychical impressions.

Again, the specific molecular influences of different bodies are correlated with motion, and may be transformed into tangible activities; activities so far removed from our ordinary conceptions of the conditions under which motion is produced, yet so demonstrably though invisibly determined by molecular influences, as to suggest a series of intelligences in apparently lumpish and inactive masses of matter.

An experiment first instituted by Dr. Leger, of London, and verified by the celebrated Dr. Philips, of Paris, bears on this point with singular felicity.

Placing a *carafe* firmly in a wooden socket, the circular limb of the vase engaged in a *rainure* or groove, from a disk of copper that closes the throat of the vase is dropped a tube of the same metal, and to the disengaged end of this is fixed an arm or bar (of copper also), furnished at one extremity with a bullet or other weight, so as to balance, and at the other with a linen thread dropped a little distance and weighted with an *olive de cire* so as to form a very delicate pendulum within the belly of the *carafe*, insulated alike from atmospheric and electrical currents, and firmly protected from possible tremor of the finger by an exact fit of the disk to the throat of the vase.

Now place the index-finger of the right hand on the upper surface of the disk, and at the same moment take a morsel of sulphur in the palm of the left. The pendulum is still immovable, and remains so for a few seconds; but an invisible motor is creeping along the copper conductor, enveloping by degrees the tube and the bar, and at last descending the linen thread, at the end of which is suspended the bit of wax, at liberty. The wax olive now trembles, oscillates at last, and finally assumes a continuous rotary motion which enlarges in diameter until it attains a fixed limit, proportionate to the volume of the sulphur. This it maintains with constant precision from left to right.

If, now, the sulphur be replaced with a piece of silver, the pendulum gradually returns to rest as the motor is exhausted; but, as the aura of the silver suffuses the disk, the tube, and the olive, the latter trembles again, begins to swing, and describes a new circle, that enlarges in proportion to the volume of the silver. But the motion in this instance is from right to left. Renew the experiment with a piece of soap, and the motion produced is not rotary, but a swing, the scope of which is proportionate to the volume, from northeast to southwest. The result in these experiments, which are the same, however frequently repeated, would not in the least be affected by inclosing the sulphur, silver, or soap, in a porcelain box, or by insulating it from the hand in any other available manner.[1]

The relation of these experiments to so-called

[1] M. Philips draws the following general conclusions from his experiments with the instruments invented by Dr. Leger:

"1. Le mouvement que l'application d'une substance détermine dans le pendule magnétoscope est toujours le même en nature et en amplitude, quel que soit le volume actuellement employé de cette substance. Ainsi l'emploi des globules homéopathiques produit un effet entièrement semblable à celui de la substance elle-même, employée en nature, dont ces globules portent le nom.

"2. Un état d'isolement complet, réalisé entre le corps de l'expérimenteur et la substance en expérimentation par des substances étrangères ne possédant en elles aucune influence marquée sur le pendule, n'altère point sensiblement les effets obtenus lors du contact immédiat. Par exemple, dans la première expérience que j'ai citée il importerait peu, pour le résultat final, que le soufre fût à nu dans la main ou qu'il y fût placé dans une boite de bois blanc ou dans un bocal de porcelaine, celui-ci fût-il hermétiquement clos."

In facts like these, and in the consideration of their bearing upon the laws of organization, or their final transformation into such laws, the reader is enabled to appreciate how narrow is the boundary that separates organic from inorganic matter—the non-living from the lowest forms of the living. It is true that the cause which determines the growth of organic beings is still a mystery; but it is known that the materials of which such beings consist are subject to the same laws as mineral matter, and that the complexity is traceable to the peculiar qualities of the carbon; and the careful student of science is scarcely at liberty to doubt that the secret will at last be discovered. The idea of life, as an *esse*, is obsolete, and must necessarily be abandoned in favor of a system regarding it as a *posse* of organic matter. Speaking scientifically, there are as many forms of life as there are kinds of organic tissue ; and when Schelling gave his definition of life, as the tendency (in matter) to individuation, he limly anticipated Herbert Spencer's great law of differentiation.

spirit-photography, and to other performances assimilated to the thaumaturgy of the ancients, I shall not stop to elucidate, as these feats are not of a kind that can properly pretend to psychic significance; although let it be remarked *en passant* that the priests of all the ancient mysteries and oracles, from the Egyptian to the Roman, and in the middle ages pupils in thaumaturgy, were selected upon the same principle as spiritual mediums to-day, namely, by their susceptibility to the phenomenon of trance—in other words, because they were epileptics. M. Salverte is in error in his assumption that the most imposing feats of the thaumaturgists were experiments in physics. On the contrary, they dip as profoundly into the department of nervo-molecular physics as the feats of Mr. Home, Mr. Foster, or Miss Fox; and there is little that is new in modern spiritualism, except its name, as careful students of the religious literature of the ancient pagan races, and of the literature of thaumaturgy and magic, need not be reminded.

Thus far the subject of aura in its general aspects, in which apparently and to the senses inert bodies exhibit properties akin to psychic in their mysterious operations.

The subject of nerve-aura is more difficult to elucidate, because less susceptible of experiment. That it is capable of transmission through conducting media, and of acting at considerable distances through the medium of the atmosphere, is proved by the facts of mesmerism and by large classes of facts collected by medical psychologists; and that it is more or less subject to the volition of the organism whence it proceeds, and partakes of volitional properties, is equally indisputable.

When, in 1784, the celebrated Jussieu, of the commission appointed by the Academy of Sciences to investigate the phenomena of mesmerism, finally reported on the subject in a masterly document, the lucid analysis and candor of which have too seldom been emulated by scientific men, separating the phenomena into four groups, the first admitting of physiological explanation, the second militating against the theory of animal magnetism, the third attributable to the imagination, and the fourth involving the presumption of a special agency in their production, he not only paved the way for the investigations that have resulted in the discovery of nerve-aura, but gave a fillip to the scientific mind in that special direction.

As to the nature of this element there is little coincidence of opinion among scientific men. That it is not identical with electricity, though correlated with it, with light, and with other forces, Helmholtz has substantially proved, in demonstrating that the transmission of voluntary impulse from the brain to the muscles is far less rapid than electrical transmission, and is perceptibly quickened in rapidity by heat, and lessened by cold. It is susceptible of sensory impression and capable of propagating the impulses of the will; but it is also susceptible of unconscious action, as illustrated in the important case of Mary Carrick. The term *aura* as it re-relates to nerve-tissue is, therefore, as in the instance of drugs and medicines, appropriated to an emanating atmosphere having the molecular properties, motor and sensory, of nervous tissue itself, though in lessened intensity.

How sensory impressions are propagated and motor impulses transmitted, is a question upon which, again, there is little coincidence among scientific men. In my own case, in one instance of well-marked clairvoyance, though within small periphery, occasioned by fever, I was distinctly conscious of being enveloped in a peripheral sensory aura, and that my impressions of environing objects originated in this aura; and in testing or questioning clairvoyant physicians and mediums, three out of seven, who had any recollection at all of what they saw or said in the clairvoyant state, confessed that their impressions seemed to come in this manner, the remaining four asserting that, though dimly conscious, they saw and said things as in a dream, and could not distinctly recall them.

It is as nearly certain, however, as the only proximately demonstrable by experiment can be, that all sensations or impressions coming by way of the optic, auditory, olfactory, gustatory, and peripheral nerves, are reflex representatives and equivalents in consciousness for molecular vibrations emanating from the bodies of which cognition is taken, and that the impressions received in the clairvoyant state have the same origin; though in the deeper and more interior order of trance, into which it finally develops, reflex excitability of the gray matter of the brain appears to be responsible for the visions so often described. I have no doubt that this existed in Poe's case, and was the principal element in those unearthly imaginings that occur in his weirder and more spiritual tales, though present limits preclude collation of the evidences tending to establish it; and Dr. J. G. Holland recently called my attention to a strange and spectral painting, executed in an interval of unconsciousness, that betrays similar traits of imagination.

But to return. The part that nerve-atmosphere plays in society and in life is important, though little comprehended. How else is it possible to account for the singular ascendency that persons of inferior intellect and ability often gain over persons of exceeding intellectual and moral superiority. Upon what other hypothesis can be explained the strange intimacy that subsisted between the intellectual Hegel and stupid Henry Beer, with his thousands of dollars invested in walking-sticks? The idol of Germany with a fool for his Pylades, to the laughter of all Berlin. True that Heyne, with his acute perception of the sarcastic aspects of the intimacy, refers it to another cause, namely, that, Beer being a fool, the philosopher could talk to him without danger of being comprehended; true that Heyne was tolerably well acquainted with Hegel. But yet his observations on this point, as elsewhere, where it is possible to turn a sarcasm, must be taken *cum grano salis*.

Our likings and our antagonisms, our inexplicable antipathies against some, our inexplicable attraction to others, are not subject to considerations of moral or intellectual altitude. I like this man, with no moral or intellectual reason for liking him. I dislike the other, with as little good reason for disliking him. Indeed, the liking often coexists with moral turpitude and unreliability, and the dislike with moral rectitude. I regard these phenomena, though some refer them to intuition, as simple nervous impressions. In the course of a lounge down Broadway, I walk through the nervous atmospheres of a thousand persons. They impress me dimly. This one repels, that one attracts; but, had I the nervous organization of a Zschokke, I would read the souls of these men and women like so many diaries of their daily lives.

I have observed and been impressed by this atmosphere in the persons of criminals to a greater extent than with any other class; and this agrees with the remark of Dr. Maudsley, that criminals as a rule are subjects of nervous disorder—how often of the reflex type is proved by the statistical observation that one criminal in a hundred is the victim of pronounced epilepsy. I could not sit within ten feet of an habitual criminal in a Fifth-Avenue parlor, without knowing it; and there are men whom I know to be insane, notwithstanding the fact that they are elegantly-dressed Broadway promenaders.

These things are not fancies. On the contrary, in conversation with an insanity expert recently, I was enabled to compare my own observations with those of a master in morbid psychology, and to discern the importance of nerve-aura as a factor in the determination of this class of cases. The question was this: " In those instances in which, so far as impulsive and morbid acts are concerned, the subject of an examination presents no indisputable evidences of insanity, upon what grounds is one person remitted to the hospital, while another is adjudged simply eccentric?" In other words, in the cases of two persons, both apparently inhabitants of the border-land, upon what evidence is it concluded that the one has passed the boundary of sanity and that the other has not? It is impossible to dissect the brain of either, and the mental and physical symptoms are perhaps parallel. Substantially the answer of the expert amounted to this: "I feel that the one subject is insane and that the other is not"—a reply apparently equivalent to saying that he knew insanity by intuition, but really scientific in its terms. In other words, to untangle a paradox, the decision in these cases is largely due to the nervous aura of the subject. The same act, the same mental eccentricity, may be sane in one man and insane in another.

Again, all organic structures have their special forms of nerve-aura. The evidences that support this hypothesis are so varied and indisputable, that it is now conceded by scientific men. Certain species of serpents, for example, are capable of fascinating birds and animals, as was long since indicated by the observations of Dr. Good, Prof. Silliman, Dr. Barrow, the South American traveler, and M. Vaillant and Mr. Bruce, the African explorers. Negroes can, it has been observed, detect the presence of a rattlesnake at the distance of three hundred feet, by the diffusion, says an eminent Carolinian observer, of an exceedingly attenuated ether that acts benumbingly on the nervous system. *Vice versa*, Mr. Bruce, from minute personal observation, distinctly states that the negroes of Sennaar are so armed by nature that they handle scorpions and vipers with perfect impunity; and Lindekranz, a Swedish *savant* of eminence, affirms that the natives of Lapland and Dalarne subdue dogs in the same mysterious manner. "I constantly observed," says the former, explaining the physiology of the process, "that, however active the viper was before he was laid hold of, he seemed to sicken and become torpid, often shutting his eyes, and never turning his fangs toward the arm of the person that held him."

I have constantly observed that epileptics, pending the incubation of the fit, appear to be enveloped in a sensitive and highly-excited nerve-atmosphere, which, sometimes accompanied with sullenness, but not seldom with exceeding sensory exaltation and with preternatural acuteness of perception, heralds the attack, or, when transformed into the larvated type by mesmeric passes, eventuates in clairvoyance and trance.

These data support the hypothesis that all nervous organisms emit an ethereal aura susceptible of control by consciousness, of transmission in a given direction at the will of the organism, and of translation into physical phenomena under given conditions. Many of those strange disturbances of the equilibrium of objects within their sphere, observed to occur in nervous maladies, are no doubt due to this element. I have seen persons, subject to nervous paroxysms, upset a glass of water without contact. Under ordinary circumstances, the balance between the bundle of forces represented by a man and those represented by the inorganic bodies that environ him, is more or less stable. On the other hand, in disorders of the epileptic type the auras of various bodies act powerfully as peripheral incitations, the nervous aura of the invalid acting with reciprocal energy on them. The force of this point will appear more particularly, if the reader will carefully study the case of Mary Carrick, which, as exhibiting both series of phenomena incident to spiritualism, the nervo-psychic and the nervo-dynamic, in nearly equal proportions, must be regarded as a typical instance.

I have memoranda of the case of a celebrated medium named Conklin, subject to well-marked attacks of cerebral epilepsy, with its faded and blood-suffused eye, cadaverous pallor, and heavy and lost expression, who illustrated the phenomenon of nervous atmosphere, and the disturbances of surrounding objects incident to the malady, to a greater extent than any person I have ever met. He had made considerable stir in Washington by predicting the assassination of Mr. Lincoln, and appeared at Dodworth Hall, New York, with a transcript of trance-observations of lunar scenery, interlarded with trance *séances;* but, owing to feebleness of physical organization, he did not excel in dynamic phenomena, though disturbances of the lesser sort, and particularly rappings, were generally present as the exponents of the clairvoyant state. I saw a glass of water fall from the desk at Dodworth Hall on one occasion, when he certainly was not within six feet of it, and no other person was within ten.

Dr. Wood, of Somers, Connecticut, a cautious scientific observer, also states that on one occasion he took the opportunity to test the clairvoyance of a young woman giving *séances* in that town, who, following the hegemony of his mind, described his own study with exceeding accuracy of detail, even to the finding of the skeleton in the closet; giving the titles of medical works, describing the binding of different volumes, and exhibiting other indications, of equally minute description, that she was in perfect *rapport*, not only with him, but with other persons within a given periphery.

Dr. Patterson, of Virginia, relates the case of a lady subject to attacks of catalepsy and lying in trance, who, one stormy night, when her physician was not expected, insisted that she saw him away off riding on horseback through the rain, and tracked him step by step thence to the door, the attendants taking it for granted that she was dreaming until a rap was heard, the door was opened, and he walked in dripping.

These facts, to which medical psychologists can add by the volume, carefully attested and collated, intimate, not only that the solution of the phenomenon known as transfer of state, or as being *en rapport*, lies in the investigation of the nature of nerve-atmosphere, but that the nervo-molecular phenomena incident to the *séances* of Mr. Home are due to the same mysterious agency, acting in mediums of vital temperament and of powerful *physique* with an energy that approximates to the superhuman.

There is nothing so very singular about this. Every act of our lives is a transformation of nervous force into motor; and that nervous force may be correlated into light is demonstrated by abundant facts. Phosphorescent animals become so under an impulse of the will, through the agency of the nervous system, evolving light as a transformation of its energy; and in some cases of consumption, witnesses that distinguished physician, Dr. Brown-Séquard, light appears at the head of the sufferer, and may even radiate from him into the room. I doubt, however, whether this occurs in cases where no latent neurosis exists, to be developed by the debility incident to the disorder.

The special origin of the sensory and motor aura concerned in these phenomena remains to be indicated. That the convulsions of epilepsy are due to reflex excitability of the nerve-centres has long been established. Dr. Hughlings-Jackson took another step in advance when he propounded the hypothesis that these nervous currents or shocks are generated by a lesion of the centres involving the phenomenon of sudden and explosive liberation of the nervous energy. This view of the origin of the shock has since been demonstrated by electrical excitation of the brain in a series of experiments carried on by Prof. Ferrier, of London; so that it is now evident that epilepsy carries with it the notion of molecular disturbance of the nervous system, and, through this, of alterations in its molecular constitution. It is specifically a nervous malady, and may coexist with great physical strength.

In this molecular disturbance of the nerve-centres, spinal or cerebral, with its periodical shocks and its currents of liberated nerve-force, must be sought, if physiological observation is not at fault, the special origin of the motor and sensory nerve-atmosphere concerned in the *séances* of mediums. That this reflex excitability may be induced by volition in cases where the predisposition exists, there is no doubt. Nor is there any doubt that it may be transformed into a nervous habit, to be, within certain limits, indulged in at will of the psychic; but, on the other hand, a period answering to the period of incubation must always, so far as I have observed, intervene between the *séances*, and during this period the medium's will and fixedness of attention are incapable of producing the fit.

Before entering upon the nervo-dynamic series described by Prof. Crookes as incident to the *séances* of Mr. Home and Miss Fox, let me, in conclusion, remind the reader that clairvoyance with its peripheral nerve-atmosphere is the constant exponent of the type of organization necessary to become a medium. Let it be observed also that in mediums of powerful *physique* it is invariably accompanied by the dynamic series, while in those of more cephalic type it rapidly develops into the deeper order of trance. Within the circle of my own observation I find not a single exception to this rule, and I have notes personally jotted of over fifty mediums, including Mr. Home, Mr. Foster, A. J. Davis, Miss Fox, Miss Emma Hardinge, a dozen women famous in trances, and thrice as many men famous in the same walk.

Let the reader now bear in mind the general relations previously developed between persons of epileptic tendency and the auras of environing bodies; also, that the dynamic series commenced with the simple molecular phenomena of rappings and table-tipping, and has been developed by regular gradations from the levitation of bodies to luminous clouds, and from luminous clouds to phantom-hands and molecular spectres, with pencils without hands writing messages by the way.

Let him remember that, though subsensible, observation and experiment seem alike to indicate that nerve-aura is material—an imponderable nervous ether, possibly related to the odyle (odic gas) not long since announced by a celebrated observer as an element of organic structures. It is thus at once a force and a medium, susceptible of control by the will of the operator, and capable of sensory impression: an atmosphere to take shape at his command, and to dissolve the moment the volition ceases, or, when the habit of the medium's will has become fixed in that direction, to come and pass in visible apparitions, without conscious subjective impulse on his part. Here, then, is the subsensible medium infolding me like a spirit, that may be caused to reflect the wildest imaginings of my own soul. And here let me venture to suggest—but only to suggest, for my observations have not been extensive enough to confirm it—that many of the hallucinations of madness, and of epileptic mania in particular, so far from being utterly unreal, are phantom-forms originated in this peripheral aura by the morbid impulses of the fit, and analogous in origin to Mr Home's apparitions, which, with his thrice-acute perception, the madman sees, though they are invisible to less excited nerves. Not often, perhaps, is this the case; but I have no doubt that this same subtile atmosphere is responsible for now and then a tale of goblin or of ghost. I know one madman who, in the exacerbations of his fit, always sees his own face a few feet from him, mocking his contortions. That you and I cannot see it, by no means proves that it is not there, but that the madman's eye is superhuman in its sight.

VI.

MEMORANDA OF NERVO-DYNAMIC PHENOMENA.

Though singularly adapted to captivate the popular imagination and to impress the nerves, this series seems to me less important than the nervo-psychic series, because its facts are in their nature more nearly allied to feats practised by the ancient magicians and thaumaturgists. For example, few of the feats of Mr. Home exceed those attested of Pirnetti, a famous conjurer, who appeared at St. Petersburg early in the present century. This Pirnetti, on the occasion of his first *séance* before the Czar Alexander, was a little dramatic in his method. The hour set was seven o'clock. Five minutes after seven, and no Pirnetti. A quarter past—no Pirnetti. Half-past seven, and no Pirnetti. Messengers went, and returned unsuccessful. The czar waxed wrathful, but no Pirnetti. At last, as all the clocks in the palace were about to strike eight, the door opened, and Pirnetti was announced and walked in with the serenity of a punctual conjurer. The emperor was just about to indulge in a burst of wrath, when Pirnetti took the initiative with the question—

"Did not your majesty command my presence at exactly seven o'clock?"

"Just so!" responded the exasperated czar.

"Well, then," said the conjurer, quietly, "let your majesty deign to consult your dial, and you will see that I am exact, and that it is just seven o'clock."

The czar consulted his dial, and was amazed. The hands marked exactly seven. All the courtiers did so in their turn, and it was seven. All the clocks in the palace were at the seven. Anger was succeeded by admiration.

"Your majesty will pardon me," said Pirnetti. "I was desirous of making an impression. If you will consult again, you will find the hands marking the real hour."

And every dial in the palace, from that in the czar's pocket and those in the pockets of the assembled courtiers to the great clocks with silver faces, indicated a few minutes past eight. As he was about leaving, having performed other equally astonishing feats, the emperor reminded Pirnetti that he had boasted that he could penetrate anywhere.

"So I can, your majesty," replied the conjurer.

"Very well," said the czar, "at twelve o'clock to-morrow I shall have ready in my closet one thousand rubles; come and get them; but I forewarn you that the doors shall be closed and carefully guarded."

"To-morrow, at noon, I shall have the honor of presenting myself before your majesty," said Pirnetti, and withdrew.

The gentlemen of the house followed the conjurer to see that he quitted the palace, accompanied him to his lodgings, and caused the house to be surrounded by a cordon of the police the moment he entered. The palace was instantly closed, with orders to suffer no one to enter until the czar commanded it. High dignitaries held every avenue to the emperor, and all the palace keys were carried into the imperial cabinet and locked up. A few minutes before twelve the minister of the police announced by message that Pirnetti had not left home.

Twelve o'clock sounded, but, while the last stroke reverberated, the door between the bedroom of the czar and his cabinet opened, and Pirnetti appeared.

He concluded his feats by leaving St. Petersburg, which then had fifteen gates, at all the gates at ten o'clock exactly. That he did so was declared by hosts of spectators who knew him by sight, and attested by the written declarations of the officers placed at the gates to inspect the passports of travelers. And the inscription of his passports was inscribed in the fifteen registers.

I relate this remarkable but well-attested story, because it serves to indicate the perfection to which conjuring has been carried, and to suggest the limits that should naturally govern inquiry into the nature of phenomena called spiritual. Prof. Crookes will probably reply that Pirnetti was a psychic; but, as he made no pretense to be more than a conjurer, it is safe to accept him at his own valuation, and scientific men cannot be justly called upon to explain that which pretends to no spiritual altitude. I shall, on this principle, omit considering all feats, like the unbinding of mediums tied with ropes, that have the flavor of trickery, or mere sleight of hand.[1]

Excluding the army of jugglers who make a profession of curious feats in the name of spiritualism,

[1] The really important phenomena associated with spiritualism are not the dynamic feats and the strange transformations incident to the *séances* of mediums, but those involving the presumption of superhuman intelligence. The former have been known for ages, and are definitively associated with the magic and mysteries of the ancients, to say nothing of jugglery in its more modern aspects; and one is scarcely called upon to explain that which is confessedly illusive. On the other hand, the more difficult series, dipping deep into the laws of life and into the profounder problems of medical psychology, presents facts worth the attention of the scientific inquirer, though the pretense of regarding them as a basis for religion has led scientific men to doubt their authenticity, and repelled them from an investigation abundant in materials calculated to result in a deeper comprehension of the import of psychology as a science. Hence, in this treatise, I have, in the main, disregarded mere *tours de force* on the part of mediums, and addressed myself to the class involving psychic facts of a type more or less inexplicable from the stand-point of the general observer, and susceptible of explanation only by special study and careful examination in all their details. It would, undoubtedly, be pleasant to the general reader to find in these pages some explanation of the various trickeries habitual to mediums of a certain class, but it would conduce nothing to the scientific value of this work.

the observed phenomena, under this series, fall naturally into six classes:

CLASS I.—The movement of heavy bodies, either with or without muscular contact, is a phenomenon now so well known as to preclude the necessity of annoting special instances. On one occasion, when a circle had been formed and several mediums were present, a slight quivering of the room was perceptible to the senses; but, generally, articles of furniture give the responses.

CLASS II.—This, one of the earliest developed, is known under the general name of rappings. They pertain to every medium I have observed, but vary considerably in quality and rhythm with different mediums. I have experimented on this class with a thin mahogany table upon which fine sand was sprinkled. With the medium seated at the end, his hands resting lightly on the table, in ten minutes after the experiment commenced, waves of molecular vibration, proceeding from the psychic, had distributed the sand in long, irregular furrows. I then requested six taps at a single point, which I designated with my finger. These were given in a cascade, visibly disturbing the sand. I regard this experiment as conclusive evidence that the rappings are purely molecular phenomena.

CLASS III.—The lifting of bodies of more or less weight also pertains to nearly every medium of the nervo-dynamic type, whose operations I have witnessed. Mr. Home excels in this class of manifestations. On one occasion, at a *séance* given by him at Stafford, Connecticut, early in his career, I saw him lift a table upon which two persons were seated, without visible contact. I was standing near him at the moment, so as to be between him and the body to be lifted. A peculiar rushing current, as of the wind, appreciably preceded the levitation. In an experiment on this phenomenon, conducted in my own room, a large back parlor, in New York City, with one of the *habitués* of Metropolitan Hall, in Sixth Avenue, I was able, by a very simple test, to refer this current to the person of the medium. Placing myself between him and the large centre-table in the middle of the room, then holding a large sheet of paper of very dense fibre before him, and between him and the article to be lifted, so as to intercept the current, if any, and awaiting the result, the sheet was visibly swayed in the direction of the table, and with considerable force. It should be added that the medium was seated between the table and the unbroken inner wall of the room, and that the windows and doors were shut. The marble top of the table only was lifted. By projecting this current downward, I have no doubt that a powerful medium might lift himself from the ground, but have never witnessed the attempt, though Mr. Home is credited with having accomplished it.

Repeating this experiment with the same medium, I discarded the paper test, and addressed my attention to the question whether the liberation of this current was attended with any physical symptoms. It was between three and four o'clock in the afternoon, and the room light enough for careful observation. Talking carelessly, but with my eyes fixed on him at a distance of about four feet, my scrutiny was rewarded by the observation of a sudden pallor suffusing his face, and a perceptible tendency to rigidity of the muscles, indicative of a nervous shock. I did not observe his eyes particularly. To this class of phenomena belong the waving of curtains, the swinging of pendulums at a distance, and the sounding of notes on a distant piano.

CLASS IV.—The phenomenon of floating luminous bodies is of later origin than the mere *tours de force* grouped together under the three preceding classes, though the correlation of nerve-atmosphere as a floating or hovering motion was witnessed by me at a private *séance* given in Bond Street, one evening in the summer of 1865, and at subsequent *séances* given by the same medium. In this instance an instrument known as the harmonicon hovered about the room, emitting musical sounds at first, then falling into a kind of accentuated rhythm of notes, which, however, did not resemble any tune with which I am familiar. In the summer of 1867, at a parlor *séance* given by a wealthy spiritualist, then resident in Thirtieth Street, a luminous nebula hovered over the piano for a moment; a cascade of notes trickled from the keys, as if an invisible hand had swept them, and then the instrument fell into

Mendelssohn's "Midsummer-Night's Dream" overture. There was no one within six feet of the piano, nor did the closest examination reveal any visible cause for the music. While the nebula was hovering over the instrument, the medium was sitting by the table, say eight feet distant, silent and motionless. The nebula, on the other hand, was pervaded with a kind of swinging and swaying motion, and, as the music ceased, it wasted away in its place. Interposing between the table and the instrument with a sheet of paper, the test was swayed toward the phantom, as by the wind. The phenomenon lasted possibly four minutes. It was an afternoon *séance*, the parlor was well lighted, and there were no facilities at hand for producing an optical illusion at the point occupied by the apparition.

In the course of the conversation that followed the *séance*, the medium stated to me that he was not a musician, and could not possibly have executed the overture; but, on inquiry, I ascertained that four persons present were acquainted with the piece. It was a little mysterious to me at that date, I confess; but, in the light of later investigation, it would not at all stagger me, if, after a similar *séance*, I should ascertain that neither the medium nor any other person present was acquainted with a piece drawn from the piano apparently by a luminous nebula; for, knowing from observation the superhuman recollection of previous impressions appertaining to these states of the nervous system, I should only conclude that the medium had heard it at some remote date, and that it had sprung up spontaneously under unnatural nervous excitation. The note-books of medical men who make nervous affections a specialty, are full of analogous instances in which faculty apparently preternatural has been developed in these nervous states. I have in my possession a piece of music arranged for the flute by a somnambulist who was no musician when he was conscious. Prof. Crookes says that, under the strictest test conditions, he has more than once had a solid, self-luminous, crystalline body placed in his hand by a hand which did not belong to any person in the room. He has also observed luminous points of light darting about and settling on the heads of different persons in the room; has had questions answered by flashes in his face; has seen sparks of light ascending from the table to the ceiling, and has been present when a solid, self-luminous body floated silently about the room, descended and thrice struck the table, and then faded away. While this was going on, the medium was lying back apparently insensible.

CLASS V.—The apparition of luminous hands writing messages with a pencil has been witnessed by so many observers, and under the strictest conditions of test, that it is not necessary more than to describe them. The observations of Dr. Holland, my own, and those of Prof. Crookes, however varied in the details, agree in one point, that a luminous nebula generally precedes the formation of the phantom. Prof. Crookes has observed this nebula gradually condense into the form of a hand, and carry small objects about. He has seen a nebula hover over a heliotrope, snap off a sprig, and present it to a lady. Robert Dale Owen relies implicitly on this class of phenomena as illustrative of spiritual presences. Prof. Crookes, who has had better opportunity of observing this class than I have, having had Mr. Home at his command for some years, gives more instances of phantom-apparition, and more satisfactory instances, than I have been able to find. He states that, on one occasion, a small hand appeared thrice at the dining-table, and handed him a flower; at another, a small hand and arm appeared playing about a lady, then patted him on the arm, and plucked at his sleeve; at another, a finger and thumb picked at the petals of a flower in Mr. Home's button-hole, and distributed them to persons sitting near him. At another, he saw a visible hand fingering the keys of an accordeon; at another, he saw an object move first, then a luminous nebula enveloped it, and gradually condensed into a hand. Frequently, these appearances look solid and life-like, the fingers moving, and the external surface of natural color, while at the wrist the hand shades off into luminous haze. They are often warm, but more generally cool. He has held one of these hands in his own until it gradually resolved into vapor and faded from his grasp. Miss Fox as medium, he has seen a luminous hand come down from above, hover near him for a few seconds, take a pencil from his hand, and rapidly write on a sheet of paper, then drop the pencil, ascend ceiling-ward, and waste into darkness. This was done under strict conditions of test.

Having rooms for some months in the spring of 1867, after my return from the country, at the house of a gentleman and his wife in Thirtieth Street, who were both enthusiastic spiritualists, and mediums of considerable faculty, I had more or less daily contact with advocates of the special tenets of spiritualism. Both my landlord and landlady, by-the-way, suffered from periodical nervous attacks. During this period, in addition to *séances* in my professional capacity, I was able to observe very minutely, in a couple of its exemplary representatives, the peculiar mental aura habitual to the class, and have learned to give but little weight to their testimony, without doubting their sincerity, but as colored and determined by nervous disorder. Scientific observation calls for a mind loyal to facts and indifferent to prejudices, acutely perceptive and skeptical, and—beyond all—unbiased by those morbid predispositions that spring from nervous perversion, either hereditary or acquired. I have, hence, with the single exception of Prof. Crookes, rejected the literature of spiritualism, in so far as it bears upon these phenomena, save when supported by my own observation, or by the word of accredited scientific witnesses—medical preferred.

At private *séances* (aside from special experiments) I have twice witnessed the phenomenon of a phantom-hand writing messages with a pencil. They were preceded by luminous vapor in both instances; and the *séances* occurred in the evening, though under conditions that rendered trickery impracticable.

In the first instance, after sitting a few minutes, the medium asked whether any one present had a pencil. I took a lead-pencil from my vest-pocket, and held it in my hand. No person present was within four feet of the centre-table, upon which lay several loose sheets of letter-paper. Presently, a luminous vapor, accompanied with perceptible motion, as of a gelid wind brushing past my hand, appeared hovering over the pencil. It did not seem to come from anywhere in the room, but to form gradually in its place from invisible materials. I did not once remove my eyes from it, though my nerves were just a little shaken. The nebulous stage had not lasted in excess of ten seconds, when the light commenced to die out at the base, and a filmy, semi-transparent hand and arm gradually grew out of it, like a transformation of the nebula itself. It did not seem to me that any particular part of the hand and arm was formed first, though near the elbow the arm became fainter and fainter, and was finally merged into luminosity. Taking the pencil from my hand, the apparition floated toward the table, and wrote on one of the loose sheets, "I have done this, that all present may know I am a spirit." The pencil dropped, the hand melted into vapor, the vapor into the invisible. That there was no writing on either of the several sheets on the table before the *séance* commenced, I know from personal examination.

At a *séance* given by the same medium two evenings later, the phenomenon was repeated; and on this occasion I gave more attention to the operator, and less to the feat. The point was, to observe whether any symptoms of nervous disturbance preceded the formation of the nebula, or were contemporaneously developed. Two seconds, I should say, before the luminous cloud appeared hovering over the table, upon which lay a pencil and some blank sheets of foolscap, four in number, a barely perceptible shudder ran through the person of the medium, who, from that instant, seemed to sink rapidly into a state resembling mild cataleptic trance, and lay in that state while the hand was writing the message: "Ye walk daily on the border of the spirit-land, yet ye deny spirits; I am the same that spoke to you on Monday evening." The pencil dropped, the hand wasted away, the medium slowly recovered from slumber. This medium was kind enough afterward to give me an afternoon at my rooms, by way of verifying the facts, and preventing trickery.

CLASS VI.—This class forms a natural appendix to the preceding, and is of still later production.

Prof. Crookes gives two instances, Mr. Home as medium in both cases, in which he has witnessed full-length phantoms under satisfactory test conditions.

It was just at twilight, in his own parlor, and the medium was sitting about eight feet from the windows, when the curtain was observed to move, and the semi-transparent form of a man was witnessed by all present. The phantom was standing by the window, and appeared to move the curtain with its hand.

In the second instance a phantom-form came from the corner of the room, took an accordion in its hand, and floated about the room for many minutes, playing the instrument. It was visible to all present. A slight cry from a lady caused it to vanish.

I have not witnessed this full-length phenomenon personally under conditions of test so accurate as to preclude possible deception.

At the *séances* of Mrs. Holmes, of Philadelphia, which I twice attended, a board partition across the corner of the rooms formed a triangular cabinet of shallow dimensions, from which examination disclosed no means of exit, except the door. The door of this cabinet opened, and a luminous nebula appeared and gradually assumed the shape of a woman dressed in the Greek fashion, wearing a lace scarf on her head, her arms bare and sleeves flowing—a very dramatic spectre indeed. The apparition floated into the room, gossiped with one, accepted a bouquet from another, returned to the cabinet, and gradually wasted into nebula, then into nothing. The spirit announced herself as Miss Katie King, daughter of John King, a pirate in the days of Robert Kidd. I did not trouble myself to apply tests in this instance, as the *séances* seemed to partake of the Pirnetti type too obviously to command investigation from the stand-point of this inquiry. Mrs. Holmes, let me add, is a person of considerable physical force.

The reader will notice at a glance that the luminous nebula is a condition precedent in the production of the phantom; and, if accustomed to scientific experiment, he will suspect that this luminosity is consequent upon molecular agitation at the point whence the light proceeds. That the nerve-ether proceeding from the person of a medium should be susceptible of condensation into a nebula, then into a phantom, is no more wonderful, though more striking, than that, as in the various nervo-psychic cases, it should be susceptible of sensory impression. Again, the peculiar nature of the luminosity developed by the nebula corresponds in all particulars with that of the light sometimes developed about the heads of epileptics at different stages of the disorder. I have not been able to attempt spectrum analysis in either case, nor are the conditions such as to render it practicable; but I have no doubt that analysis, were it possible, would show that they are identical; and no person, who has witnessed both, could have any reasonable doubt on the subject. It may be possible, by-and-by, to demonstrate this point by instrumental tests of absolute accuracy; but so evanescent are the conditions, so feeble often is the luminosity developed by nerve-ether, that the world will have to wait long for an unerring demonstration of what is undoubted. I have had many opportunities of comparing the two, and I cannot be mistaken as to a luminosity so peculiar in its quality and behavior as that of nerve-atmosphere under excitation. Could this point be demonstrated by absolute instrumental tests, the whole question—whether these phantoms are or are not transformations of nervous ether—would be settled beyond the need of physiological induction.

At a *séance* given me one afternoon at my rooms, by the same medium whose private *séances* I attended, removing the arm of a horseshoe magnet, I brought the open poles in contact with the nebula, with a view of testing whether it could be dissipated in that way. The test was not successful from that aspect of the subject; but it was quite successful from another point of view that seems to me equally conclusive. The poles of the magnet being advanced toward the border of the nebula, the medium, who was sitting about six feet from it, apparently half asleep, was attacked with perceptible convulsions of tetanic cast. On closing the armature, the convulsions ceased. Though not dissipated by magnetism, the nebula also was perceptibly agitated to and fro, and developed augmented light. I now tested the matter further, by removing the arm of the magnet at other points in the room contiguous to the medium, but no perceptible effect on his nerves was developed. I regard this test as conclusive evidence that the nebula was in this case a transformation of the nervous atmosphere of the medium, and that the magnetism that produced the slight spasms was transmitted to the medium's nerves through contact with this nervous nebula, suspended in the atmosphere fully six feet from his person. At a subsequent experiment with the same medium, the same phenomena were repeated upon removing the arm of the magnet in contiguity to the cloud. The magnet was one capable, possibly, of lifting twenty pounds.

This test is not, perhaps, so unerring as a test more instrumental in its nature would be, but it seems to me conclusively to establish the nervous constitution of the nebula.

Two *séances* were afterward given me at my rooms in West Twenty-fourth Street, New York, by another medium of considerable pretensions, at both of which messages were written by phantom-hands on sheets of foolscap lying on the large centre-table, the medium sitting about six feet from the table, on the sofa. In both instances the luminous mist preceded the hand by some seconds. One of these messages I find in my note-book as a transcendental aphorism worthy of Mr. Ralph Waldo Emerson. It reads, "Matter and soul are the two poles of one and the same infinite reality." The other is a singular definition of trance, and runs, "By trances the soul partakes of the life infinite." I will note as a curious fact that both these messages, though I had never had any conversation with the medium on the subject, were but verbal deliveries of two ideas which had been running in my mind for some months, and which had already been elaborated in literary form. One of them was afterward printed in the *Radical* for April, 1871, published in Boston, as a criticism on the speculative tendencies of Herbert Spencer, Huxley, Bain, and other leading exponents of scientific thought in England. Nor have I any doubt that the origin of the messages in both instances was due to my own studies in that special direction.

Tested, in the first instance, with a magnet brought in contiguity to the half-vapory hand, while in the act of writing, the medium, half reclining on the sofa, suddenly started up rigidly, and sank back upon the withdrawal of the current, which, however, did not extinguish the apparition, although the pencil staggered perceptibly. Tested similarly in the second instance, the effect was less marked, both on the medium and on the spectre; and I was again unsuccessful in my attempt to extinguish the phantom with a magnet, though the pencil wavered slightly with the current, and resumed its regularity upon withdrawal, and a slight but visible tremor was its exponent in the nervous system of the operator, who subsequently confessed that he experienced something like a shock on the application of the poles to the edge of the half-condensed nebula, just above the wrist, but attributed it to the *rapport* between himself and the spirit. The magnet was the same as that employed in the former experiments.

Thus, though any actual comparison of analyses of these phenomena—the light developed in epilepsy and that developed in the luminous nebulæ at spiritual *séances*—is impracticable, no reasonable doubt can exist as to the nervous origin of the phantoms quoted by spiritualists as demonstrative of actual spiritual agency in human affairs.

The main difficulty that will occur to the general observer in this relation will be this: "Can it be that, without other conducting medium than the atmosphere, a force can be directed to a particular point and express itself in a particular form?" This difficulty is obviated by the nature of nerve-atmosphere, considered as an agent acting externally to the medium. There is no known manner in which electricity can be acted upon and controlled by volition; but in nervous atmosphere the physiologist is dealing with an agent the very nature of which is related to volition, and correlated with it. It is necessary, therefore, in the consideration of this question, to dismiss all conventional ideas on the subject of force, and to appreciate the fact that in these phenomena the investigator is engaged with a force that is, to some extent at least, self-directive and self-directing, but one not at all presuming psychic or spiritual agency external to the medium; a force that is not to be regarded as separate from other forces illustrated in the phenomena of Nature, but nevertheless self-determinative and susceptible of correlation into volition.

That these transformations of nervous atmosphere are abnormal, no physiologist doubts; but the inductions of physiology rob them of their supernatural attitude, and they present themselves to the mind of the inquirer in the aspect of strange phenomena, indicative, not of peculiar spiritual gifts, but of the possession of hereditary or acquired nervous perversion; not of possession by devils, or by spirits good or evil, as was anciently supposed, but of an inheritance of suffering and of morbidness. Let me now interpose a paragraph, and recur to this aspect of the subject further on.

C. H. Foster, native of Salem, Massachusetts, about forty years of age, of heavy and somewhat sensual face and *physique*, became clairvoyant at ten years of age. He was at first only a local celebrity, but finally traveled through the principal States of the Union. He was during his sojourn in England the guest of Bulwer, and furnished the original of Margrave in the "Strange Story." One of his feats, in which he differs from all mediums I have met in the progress of this investigation, consists in causing the initials of the spirit, supposed to be present, to appear in red letters on his hand or arm. His capacity for the performance of physical feats is perceptibly affected by atmospheric conditions. Inquiry at Salem develops the fact that he undoubtedly inherited nervous disturbance from his paternal ancestor.

Viewed in their medical aspect, the foregoing phenomena present themselves as examples of hypercinesia, the nervo-psychic series previously instanced presenting so many examples of hyperæsthesia, as the term is employed by medical psychologists. The one is associated with lesion of the motor, the other with lesion of the sensory centres. The record abounds with instances in which transformations of tissue have occurred as the sequels of intense nervous impression. A young lady in Geneva, Switzerland, whose mistress had died under operation for cancer, and who was similarly afflicted, was so overcome with terror on learning the death of her employer, that she fell down in a swoon and did not recover for some hours. When, at last, she came to herself again, the tumor had totally disappeared. A woman in Valois, afflicted with an enormous goitre, was informed by the surgeon that she would have to submit to an operation for its removal on the following day; but, when twenty-four hours afterward he presented himself, prepared for the operation, the goitre no longer existed. These, and other instances analogous to the phenomena in Mr. Foster's case, though generally classed as the products of intense action of the imagination, are

MEMORANDA OF NERVO-DYNAMIC PHENOMENA. 155

properly examples of the transforming activity of intense nervous impression. Instances of this special type need not be multiplied, for there is no dispute among scientific men as to the authenticity of the facts, although their explanation is to be sought in the molecular influence as exercised upon living tissue by nervous impression, rather than in any direct action of the imagination. The principal phenomena in Foster's case fall so obviously under this category as to preclude the necessity of other explanation than a mere request to the reader to collect, collate, and consider the many facts of this class, that medical men have observed and recorded. I cannot, however, although not strictly relevant to the discussion, resist the temptation to remind Mr. Cox and Prof. Crookes that the psychic-force theory is a plagiarism. When the interest in mesmerism was at its highest in America, between the years 1845 and 1850, a Hindoo priest named Lehanteka, then resident in California, disseminated a theory that anticipates the view taken by these gentlemen, by some years. According to Lehanteka, the perceptive and dynamic energy of man is separable into three concentric spheres; the first consisting of the sensory and motor organism; the second, of physical agents having the quality of conducting sensory and motor influences; the third, of a psychic and subsensible medium, susceptible of being acted upon by the volition of the mesmerist. One thing is known, as to the genesis of mesmeric clairvoyance, namely—that the operator acts upon his subject by means of vibrating waves of nervous atmosphere. This is experimentally demonstrated. It is also experimentally demonstrated that molecular vibrations of a given wave-length, whether acting upon the optic, olfactory, gustatory, auditory, or peripheral nerves, have a tendency to produce insensibility, and to eventuate in that morbid nervous state whence spring trance and clairvoyance. In self-induced clairvoyance, however, the medium frequently depends upon the physiological action of lifting the eyes at an angle, and retaining them in that position. This fact suggests a curious problem, and one I will not attempt to settle. In instances of trance, or insensibility, supervening after epileptic convulsions, and in most morbid nervous states, this position of the eyes (rolled up under the upper lid) is an ever-present symptom; so that the question presents itself, whether the physiological action of rolling the eyes and retaining them fixedly in that position is due to a deeper law of association than has yet been observed and stated by psychologists, or whether it is due to the direct effect of unnatural tension on the optic nerves and ganglia. Let it be noted, however, that the facts of mesmerism, so far as investigated, tend to this hypothesis: *That all these morbid states of consciousness are the exponents of molecular transformations going on in the nervous system;* and it will not be disputed, perhaps, that the normal function of any given tract of tissue, nervous or muscular, is only another name for normal molecular activity in that tract. This is the nearest proximate definition of function that physiologists can offer. Now, how is mesmeric slumber usually produced? By transverse passes from the coronal region of the brain in a generally sloping and downward direction. In other words, the manipulation tends to produce morbid function of the cortex of the brain, by means of transverse waves of molecular vibration. In this morbid condition, as previously indicated in the course of this inquiry, *the nervous system accepts and correlates as intelligence the varied operations of the molecular force instrumental in environing natural phenomena.* I have notes of one instance in which a clairvoyant predicted the fall of a manufactory, the floors of which rested upon iron columns, which, as is well known, are subject to transformations of molecular constitution through the vibratory action of continuous jar, and stated the operating cause of the catastrophe to be the effect of jar upon the iron columns; and the prediction was verified to the day and hour. I must, however, before entering specially upon the discussion of the intelligence associated with hypercinesia, put the reader in possession of a few memoranda, furnishing inductive proof that, in all its various aspects, this phenomenon is constant in its association with the epileptic aura—that is to say, with hereditary neurosis. In one case—the family well known in social circles—the daughter was subject to attacks of clairvoyance, and, being of cerebro-vital temperament, presented, to a nearly equal extent, both classes of phenomena, the nervo-psychic and the nervo-dynamic; while the son was subject to epileptic fits of pronounced type. Of three brothers, two were noted in the phenomena of table-tipping and rappings, while the third and youngest was the victim of periodical epileptic mania. Indeed, without wasting words in particularities, I will here affirm, once for all, that in no case, so far as I have examined, where one member of a family is a spiritual medium, and presents, in pronounced form, the nervous phenomena associated with spiritualism, will the careful observer find it difficult to detect and verify the existence of the epileptic predisposition in other members. The reader will understand that the preceding remarks refer only to actual nervous phenomena, and not to the optical spectres and illusions (often introduced at *séances*) dependent upon the refraction, reflection, and absorption of light—striking and interesting, as experiments in physics, but readily solved by application of known laws of optics.

VII.

PHYSIOLOGY OF THE VOLITION AND INTELLIGENCE INVOLVED IN THE FOREGOING SERIES.

SUBMITTING the facts of the preceding series to careful analysis—and they are classified in the general order of their historical succession, from the first crude rappings of the Fox sisters to the full-length phantoms of Mr. Home—the reader will observe that in the first three classes, nerve-atmosphere or nervous force is correlated with motor force in its simpler aspects, while in the last three it is correlated with light and with complex molecular phenomena of a spectral cast. He will observe also that the phenomena of all classes are continually associated with an intelligence.

The experiments described in the course of the preceding classification and description leave no room for doubt as to the immediate nervous connection that exists between the medium and his phantom, or as to the energy engaged in its production proceeding directly from the medium's person. Nor is there any doubt as to the strictly nervous origin of this energy.

The phenomenon known among spiritualists as spirit materializing itself—taking no note of the paradox involved in the phrase—results, therefore, and demonstrably, from the nervous atmosphere of the medium (that is to say, from waves of nervous ether emanating from his person and controlled by his volition), entering into intimate molecular relation and contact with surrounding bodies, gaseous as well as solid; and, could these so-called psychics be persuaded to submit the phenomena to a scientific investigation extensive and protracted enough for the purpose, there is no doubt that the field would afford new and valuable contributions to psychology. Under ordinary conditions of the nervous system, this phenomenon cannot occur, because the function of nervous force terminates in muscular coördination, and in the expression of intelligence; but, when reflex excitability, with its consequent emission of nervous energy, exists as a condition precedent, the human organism, as physicians well know, seems to be gifted with superhuman faculties. I have not met Mr. Home since I was a boy—he visited Stafford, Connecticut, in those days as an itinerant medium, and lived with an acquaintance of mine for some weeks—but I have ample testimony that at that date he was subject to nervous attacks of considerable intensity, from Mr. Amos Harvey, since deceased, an ardent spiritualist, at whose house his *séances* were given, and from inquiry at Lebanon, Connecticut, where his boyhood was passed; and in his personal appearance, as I remember him, he presented all the symptoms I have since learned to associate with the epileptic aura.

It must not be understood, however, from the general drift of the facts described in these pages, that every medium is subject to epileptic paroxysms, though many a celebrated medium has been at some period of his life, but that the nervous phenomena exhibited at *séances* replace, and are in the nature of paroxysms; being, if the phrase may be permitted, larvated forms of the malady, induced within certain limits at will, but only after a more or less prolonged period of incubation. The case of Dr. Newton, a well-known healing medium, whose exhibitions I have attended on several occasions, presents an example of this principle. Although of powerful *physique*, and of strongly-marked vital temperament, during his intervals of rest the faculty is quite passive, not from muscular exhaustion, but from the fact that reflex excitability cannot be set up at will until a period of incubation has been passed.

It has been stated that nervous force may be correlated into motor force and into light. It should be added that it may be correlated into electricity and converted into the shock, as occurs in the instance of electric fishes, in which no physiologist doubts that the shock is contingent on the volition of the animal, and produced through the agency of the nervous system. Indeed, Dr. Philips, of Paris, in his notes on this subject, entitled "La Théorie de la Sensation Extra-Nerveuse," makes this correlation the basis of what is known to ancient superstition as the faculty of second sight, and maintains that, under certain very sensitive conditions of the optic nerve, the waves of terrestrial electricity, permeating all bodies, traversing all spaces, may affect the retina of the eye; a view of the subject quite in harmony with the experimental facts that a strong current produces the sensation of a dull, red light, and that the human body may be lighted by electricity so as to reveal its organic structure.

With this point let me dismiss this aspect of the subject. There is electricity enough in a single drop of water, says Faraday, to produce a flash of lightning, could its equilibrium but be disturbed; and there is the nerve-force in a single centre of the brain to lift a hundred tons, or produce a thousand phantoms at once, could it suddenly be correlated as motor energy under the direction of the will.

As to the intelligence apparently governing these phenomena, the reader, who has carefully examined the series of cases designated as nervo-psychic, will be troubled with no doubts as to its origin in the peripheral aura that envelops the medium.

Take, for example, the principal instance depended upon by Prof. Crookes, as establishing the agency of an intelligence disconnected from the brain of the medium. During a *séance* with Mr. Home, a

PHYSIOLOGY OF VOLITION AND INTELLIGENCE. 163

small lath moved across the table to him, and delivered a message by tapping his hand, he repeating the alphabet, and the lath tapping at the right letters. The other end of the lath rested on the table. He now propounded the question, " Can the intelligence governing the motion of this lath alter the movements, and give me a telegraphic message through the Morse alphabet, by taps on the hand?" —as he had every reason to believe that the Morse code was quite unknown to any other person present, and it was only imperfectly known to him. No sooner had he said this, than the alphabetic system was abandoned, and the message was continued in the manner requested. The professor accepts this test as conclusive.

Had Prof. Crookes examined the psychology of the subject as carefully as he has the phenomena, he would scarcely have quoted this instance as supporting his view, since it is established by abundant facts and experiments—see cases VII., VIII., and IX., and the experiments of Dr. Wood—that, in the clairvoyant state, the medium becomes *en rapport* with the nervous systems of all persons within the circle of his peripheral atmosphere, whether immediately present or not. He may even (as in the case of Zschokke) know vividly that which lies dormant in their memories, and which they could not recall distinctly by any effort of the will, but which is, nevertheless, distinctly registered in the brain; and as showing how every nervous impression of our lives is actually registered and becomes a part of the brain, how often is it that a man tries to recollect, but cannot, something he is perfectly conscious of knowing. He is perfectly conscious, too, what it is that he wants to remember; puts his hand to his forehead as if to shut out external impressions while he hunts for it; and, when at last he finds it, he identifies it at once as the very thing he was looking for.

Again, the brain, as an organic register of nervous impressions, is crowded with memoranda of things that have escaped consciousness altogether. Persons subject to attacks of cerebral epilepsy tell me that, in the nervous excitability that precedes the fit, they often remember things that are to them as if they had happened in another life.

Mr. Crandall, an acute observer in these matters, states that he once called upon a clairvoyant in the western part of the State of New York, who, among other things, described his horse, one that he had recently bought, the stable where he kept it, even to the lock on the door, the blanket he had strapped over it that very morning, and—what is strangest of all—a certain minute white spot, of the existence of which he did not know. He contradicted her as to this fact; but, on repairing to the stable, careful inspection convinced him that the woman was right. The bearing of this incident is obvious. Though the impression made on the retina of the eye, and thence transmitted to the brain, had been so minute as to elude consciousness, it was, nevertheless, unconsciously registered in his nervous organism, with which the woman was *en rapport*.

To put the conclusion in a word, our nervous systems daily register thousands of impressions that are never correlated as consciousness at all, and many more that are only correlated as flitting and fantastic fancies. Never correlated, did I say? I should say never correlated, except in those strange moods when a man is clairvoyant, not only as to the world, but as to that which lies within himself.

The application of these facts to the case instanced by Prof. Crookes is obvious; so obvious that I hesitate to trouble the reader by stating it formally. As *en rapport* with his nervous system, in which, though imperfectly correlated as memory, was registered the impression of the Morse code, Mr. Home received, through the impression of his nervous atmosphere, and correlated in his own brain, with the minuteness and rapidity incident to reflex excitability, the details of that register. Strictly speaking, it is unscientific, because in excess of the necessary induction of the facts, to assume that in these states mind is *en rapport* with mind, soul with soul. On the other hand, it is nervous system that is *en rapport* with nervous system. The nervous register of a given thought in your mind is transferred to my brain as an impression of the nerve-atmosphere surrounding me, and there correlated as thought.

I would not be understood, however, as assuming that the majority of mediums are guilty of intentional deception, or that they have penetrated the scientific aspects of the subject deeply enough to have gathered the facts necessary to form a correct conclusion. With few exceptions, they are ignorant and unlettered men, who find themselves in possession of a strange faculty of trance—something that has been associated for ages with revelation and with the supernatural [1]—something that really is preternatural in some of its aspects. They dream dreams, and the dreams are fulfilled; in strange moods they have premonitions, and they come to pass. With the vast discoveries of medical psychology they are wholly unacquainted, and it never occurs to them, until too late, that these trances and dreams and premonitions and nervous shocks, as if some spirit were taking possession of them, are the exponents of nervous disorder. This, in a few words, is the history of nearly every medium I have met in the progress of this investigation; and in the mental history of most spiritualists, who are not mediums, I find the same sad struggle with a predisposition,

---

[1] There are ample reasons for concluding that the demoniac possession of the ancients was, in the main, associated with the various types of epileptic insanity. A better and more graphic description of an attack of *grand mal* could scarcely have been given by a modern physician than that of the young man possessed of a dumb spirit (Mark ix. 17, 18.) The descriptions of Luke are even more explicit. The Greeks seem to have been the only ancient race who regarded insanity as a physical disorder.

whence arising they know not. Acquit them, then, with a few exceptions, of intentional deceit, and give them pity for blame.

An instance of the singular manner in which nervous impressions are sometimes correlated into consciousness, that occurred to me in the summer of 1863, is in point here. Having taken a severe cold, I called on my doctor, who prepared me some powders, without explaining their constitution, and ordered me to take one at night before going to bed. I did as directed, and slowly recovered, the process occupying a week or more. I had never knowingly taken any opium, and was unacquainted experientially with its physiological effect; but, as the illness wore off, I commenced to have an unconquerable longing for something that expressed itself in my mind as morphia, though I had never, so far as I knew, taken any. So importunate was the passion, that I procured some morphia in doses of a quarter of a grain. After taking a dose the longing was stilled, and did not recur until the following evening, when I sopped it to sleep with another quarter. This was continued for a couple of weeks, until the habit was somewhat settled, when, one night, as I was about to swallow my usual dose, I mastered myself with a strong effort, threw my powders into the wash-basin, and vowed not to renew them. The struggle that followed was a desperate one, but I took no more morphia. Now, how should it happen that, after taking morphia, in conjunction with other agents for a few nights, unknowing what I did, the lassitude occasioned by its withdrawal should express itself in an intelligent longing for that deadly drug, except by way of that organic but generally unconscious intelligence that appertains to nervous organization?

Again, in the production of nervo-dynamic phenomena, the medium, in the semi-, or proximately complete, unconsciousness of the state, is not aware of exercising his volition; so true it is that in many of these abnormal nervous paroxysms a man seems to be a double man, even to himself. But here the stereotyped view of volition is at fault. As an energy pertaining to the motor tracts of the nervous system, volition is an element of nervous organization, and may, as is observed in somnambulism, act without the consciousness of acting.

And here I must dissent from the view of Dr. Carpenter, master of physiology in its relation to psychic states though he is; for my own observations, prosecuted for the last ten years in this special field, have convinced me that in the state known as unconscious cerebration it is not altogether habit that coördinates the muscular movements and the various acts done in unconsciousness. On the other hand, the facts point to the conclusion that, while ordinarily volition is set in motion by consciousness, it is nevertheless true that consciousness is an aspect of volition, not volition of consciousness, and that, in the state of unconsciousness, cerebration, movements and actions are intelligently though unconsciously coördinated.

In a fit of somnambulism, a clergyman repairs to his study at night, and writes his sermon; in an attack of the same, a man, unaccustomed to musical composition, produces a piece arranged for the flute, that he could no more have composed in his waking senses than he could have made a pair of wings grow from his shoulders; stunned so as to be insensible, a man walks home, undresses, and gets in bed—and never knows how he came there when he comes to himself. In either of these three acts there is volition, and in the former two, at least, it is directed by intelligence, though the intelligence is wholly unconscious. It is obvious that in madness the nervous impressions are not correlated as consciousness—else the madman would remember his madness as one remembers a dream—but madmen often display the keenest intelligence and the most marvelous fecundity of invention; not mere cunning, but invention that would have added to the fame of a Dickens. I cannot stop to discuss the varied relations that this question has to morbid psychology. Only the one point, that will and intelligence may both act without correlation as consciousness—that, consequently, both will and intelligence may be in operation on the part of the medium, without the least consciousness of it, though at *séances* the wonder-worker is usually but semi-somnolent—is of importance here. Nervous tissue lives only as having the quality of irritability self-determined. This is its life and the germ of intelligent volition. In the nervous organism of a man this tissue is differentiated into sensory and motor tracts. To a single tract—the cortex of the brain—consciousness is limited; but it must not be supposed, and need not be, that, when this function is in temporary suspension, there is, therefore, a suspension of intelligent volition. In instinct, which in its lower forms is the simplest and most rudimentary aspect of intelligent volition that observation supplies, this fundamental activity of the nervous tissue may be studied in its most interesting aspects. Our own instincts are not always, nor often, correlated into consciousness; yet they present the phenomena of selection and discrimination as to means and ends, and carry with them an unconscious understanding. A good definition of instinct would be organic intelligence, unconscious, but none the less selective and discriminative. If the reader will take the trouble to dissect any one of the great ganglia of the human body he will find them differing from the brain in no important particular, except that of an organization less complex. They are so many brains working unconsciously, but discriminatively.

The conclusion naturally flowing from these facts, and from many more, the bearing of which it seems to me that Dr. Carpenter, in his theory of unconscious cerebration, and George Henry Lewes, in his theory of instinct, have overlooked, is that the life of nervous tissue is self-determining, and that whenever this tissue is present the fundamental principle of intelligence is also present.[1] It is evident, therefore, that self-directed volition is a primary property of nervous organization.

The reader now sees how it is that the will of a spiritual medium may intelligently yet unconsciously act in the production of so-called spiritual phenomena; also, how it is that nerve-atmosphere, invisible, imponderable, but entering into intimate molecular relation and contact with surrounding bodies and with surrounding nervous organisms, is

[1] This observation cannot be properly restricted to nervous tissue, for, wherever animal tissue is present, there is present the fundamental activity that in higher organizations presents itself as conscious intelligence; and in a general way it is known that, by strict law of differentiation, nervous tissue was evolved from the lower types, and this is true without going back to the fundamental basis of life, that which forms the original stuff of all living tissues, protoplasm. Ignoring the latter, and commencing the investigation with organisms of some little complexity, it is a demonstrable fact that conscious intelligence comes through successive differentiations of a mother-tissue; for, feeling his way down the scale, the physiologist finally loses all traces of the nervous system, then all traces of bony structure, then all traces of muscular structure, until he at last encounters mere aggregations of a jelly-like substance, scarcely distinguishable as living, yet the mother-tissue of all living beings, however complex in structure, however wonderful in intelligence. The conclusion from the larger inductions of physiology is, therefore, that every ounce of tissue in the human body, of whatsoever kind or function, contributes its share in determining and giving direction to the intellectual and emotional life, and that what is generally termed instinct is a purely organic intelligence, unconscious, but competent to the special life of the organism in which it occurs.

susceptible both of sensory impressions and of motor impulses. He sees how it is that, as in the case of Florence Cook, a person in trance may produce a visible phantom and control its movements, or may even visit a person, living at considerable distance, as an apparition, write a message, and float away or waste into the invisible. I have among my memoranda no observed instances of this phenomenon; but Robert Dale Owen, in his "Footprints on the Boundary of Another World," relates an instance of it, in some respects analogous to the case of Captain Densmore, the authenticity of which there is no occasion to doubt. How wonderful our unconscious operations are—far more wonderful than our conscious—facts daily indicate to the observer who studies human life in its deeper psychological aspects; also, how superficial it is to fly to spiritual agencies, or to presumptions like the psychic-force theory, to furnish the explanation of phenomena purely incident to morbid nervous states.

Although the discussion of this aspect of the subject should properly end with the foregoing paragraph, I cannot forbear noticing a single point of physiology that dips still deeper into the *rationale* of the nervous phenomena associated with spiritualism. If, as experiments thus far seem to indicate, the functional distinction between the two classes of nervous tissue, the white and the gray, is rudimentary, the former appropriated to the propagation of motor impulses and of impressions, the latter to cognition and consciousness, then man is a double man in his nervous structure: a being of gray nerves that thinks and feels and wills, and an unconscious being of white nerves that communicates and obeys; and his psychological organism can be dissected, first, from the general nervous organism of his unconscious life, with which it is coextensive, and, secondly, from the physical organization with which it is intimately interwoven. Reasoning in and in, or rather dissecting in and in, the physiologist thus finally encounters a gray nervous spectre that thinks and feels and longs, wills and determines and controls, and constitutes the last limit of physiological induction in the direction of the spiritual. It is in this gray spectre that the blind promptings of our animal lives are correlated as emotion or as thinking—as consciousness.

Try to imagine this ultimate nervous man in which our higher energy is resident, and you but haunt your dreams with a thin and filmy ghost, that confronts you night and day in the image of yourself—matter's final *Doppelgänger* of what you feel to be the inner psychic man. For myself, I frankly confess that this gray, filmy shadow is seldom absent from my reveries. On the other hand, by some strange law of life, you find it just as impossible to identify this nerve-spectre with the ultimate psychical reality that constitutes your final self, as it is to identify muscle with the mind that moves it. It is to this nerve-spectre of ourselves, in its states of reflex excitability, that physiological investigation finally traces that motor and sensory aura that forms the scientific basis of the phenomena termed spiritual.

Tracing the two gray middle strands of the spinal axis into the brain, the physiologist finds them expanded into the two olivary bodies, and into masses of gray matter penetrated by white fibres, and finally into an intricately convolved membranous envelope termed the cortex. In the frontal and inferior portions of this gray cerebral envelope are situated various nerve-centres coördinating voluntary motion and the outward expression of intelligence. This has been proved (as before observed) by electrical excitation of the brain-envelope at the hands of Prof. Ferrier; and I may add, without egotism, that in experiments with the brains of dogs, cats, rabbits, squirrels, and other animals attainable for the purpose, I have verified Prof. Ferrier's conclusions in all important particulars. In the coronal and central region of the brain the tissue gives no muscular response to the electrical current; in a similar manner, making a deep incision so as to connect the current with either of the olivary bodies, an experiment calling for exceeding delicacy of manipulation, no muscular exponents seem to follow electrical excitation: so that it is evident from experiment that the final cognitive tract of the brain lies here, and that reflex excitability of this tract is concerned in the indrawn and strangely introspective trances of epileptics like Swedenborg. This is intellectual epilepsy in its subtilest form, as illustrated in the cases of M. Cazotte and Judge Edmonds, and by no means necessarily involves complete unconsciousness of external occurrences. The superhuman cognition that occurs in this special type of the disorder is exemplified in the case of Captain Densmore, and in those strange previsions that have been passingly discussed in a preceding section.

On the other hand, in the dynamic phenomena, incident to the *séances* of Mr. Home, the motor and medullary centres appear to be the principal seat of reflex excitability.

To return. The reader is now satisfied, I think, that the nervous state termed clairvoyance is the centre around which all the phenomena of spiritualism, psychic as well as dynamic, naturally group themselves; also, that reflex excitability of the nerve-centres constitutes the physiological basis of this state, and that in vital temperaments it develops motor aspects, while in cerebral temperaments it develops the singular sensory phenomena described in the nervo-psychic series; furthermore, that this state is the constant exponent of the epileptic neurosis.

I find no exception to this view of the case in the more than fifty mediums of whom I have collected memoranda; and, without indulging in any unpleasant criticism, I must be permitted to say that the association of either class of facts with the agency of departed spirits is quite unwarranted and gratuitous. Neither the sensory nor the dynamic phenomena of spiritualism presume intelligences or forces not explainable by physiology. I must ask scientific men, however, calmly to investigate the facts incident to these nervous states, and to assimilate them to systematic psychology — a task calling for the limits of a volume.

Beyond these states, and perhaps in that ultimate psychical body that was present to the vision of St. Paul and participates in the supersensible reality, lie our real spiritual man and the proper sphere of religion. With this reality, faith—the highest emotion of which our natures are capable—is our active contact.

So, then, if at all, our transfiguration comes by faith, not by epileptic trances. There are occasions, no doubt, when our faculties seem for the moment to be unconditioned, and our souls listen vaguely to mystic music; when the supersensible is visible through a blur, and the imagination dimly apprehends the higher beautiful. Glimpses these of our undeveloped lives, that serve to indicate to ourselves, though in the nature of things unverifiable, how diametrically these undeveloped lives differ from the cog-wheel speculations and morbid sensorial impressions illustrated in the literature of clairvoyance, from Swedenborg, its most gifted modern exponent, to Davis, Burkmar, and Tarbox, its more famous American representatives. Our lives, by dint of the undeveloped that lies within them, prophesy vaguely always. What wonder, then, if they occasionally forebode in very distinct terms?—

PHYSIOLOGY OF VOLITION AND INTELLIGENCE. 177

"The dream of ancient saints hath thus the pith
And mystic meaning of a Pindaric myth;
A strange, sweet poem fancifully wrought
Unto the current of an inner thought,
Whereby, as half-unfolded undertone,
The dim and mystic permeates the known,
And all the common things of life are linked
Unto a music strange and indistinct."

In concluding this section, permit me to add that my own observations have led me insensibly during the last ten years to the opinion that, in its motor aspects particularly, the nervous conditions necessary to so-called spiritual phenomena coexist generally with a low type of physical organization, and, with very few exceptions, the same criticism applies to mediums of the sensory class; facts sufficing in themselves to disconnect both classes of phenomena from the higher spiritual activities of human nature. But, what the real nature of nerve-aura is, can only be described by the term nerve-aura. It is not electrical, though it may be correlated as electricity; it is not psychic, though it may be correlated into apparently psychic phenomena.

Very likely, however, some clever scientific man will one of these days invent an auroscope, by which it will be possible to test the relative capacities of mediums, and to distinguish between motor and sensory, without putting them to the trouble of *séances:* and, in the observations thus far submitted, I have sought to get together the materials and experiments necessary to an exact scientific demonstration of the subject. What is wanted now is, that some scientific professor, or some medical psychologist, having the opportunity to study it in all its attitudes, should experiment and observe carefully as to the action and reaction of nerve-ether with various bodies, until such an instrument can be constructed as to determine its presence by an unerring test. Then, let this auroscope be applied to one of Mr. Home's phantoms, or to those of Mrs. Jenny Holmes, of Philadelphia, by way of determining the constitution of the former and the genuineness of the latter; and the demonstration will be as complete from the stand-point of exact physics as it seems to me from the stand-point of physiology.

VIII.

A GLANCE AT THE HIGHER RELATIONS OF THE SUBJECT.

THAT the method of criticism applied in the preceding sections, with whatever inadequacy of hand —and our best in all these matters falls lamentably short of our striving—is the true method to apply to all psychological phenomena, there has been no doubt for these many years. Turner's critics have applied it to him, with the result of giving some adequate idea of the man and his artistic products, in their mutual relation. All criticism in literature and music, and in the drama, that is valuable and lasting, possesses these qualities in proportion as it applies the physiological method with an accurate insight and an enlightened comprehension. A criticism on Shakespeare, really thorough and profound, yet remains to be written, because all his critics, Coleridge not excepted, have written with certain static and stereotyped ideas of dramatic art. Even Goethe is open to rebuke in this aspect of the case,* deep as his insight was, and pervading as was his reverence for Nature. Says a German, whose works are full of wisdom:

> "*Erkenne, Freund, was er geleistet hat,*
> *Und dann erkenne was er leisten wollte;*"

and this, taking *leisten* in its deeper sense, as the inner wishing of the author's nature and organization, comprehends, in a few words, the alphabet of a method of criticism, novel in this volume only in its application to so-called spiritual phenomena, and but comparatively novel even here—for Dr. Maudsley has, as heretofore stated, successfully though briefly applied it to the case of Swedenborg's clairvoyance and trance-revelations. It yields its finest results, however, in tracing the literature of strange natures, like Poe and Hawthorne, Dumas and Baudelaire, Goethe and Heyne, Goldsmith and Byron, not to mention many more, down to the secret wishings of the organizations whence it sprang; but it must be carefully guarded from the excessive generalizing tendency that M. Taine ingrafts upon it in his brilliant but superficial and unthoughtful volumes. That which makes Mr. Carlyle what James Russell Lowell styles him, the profoundest critic of this century in history and literature, is due to the unconscious but singularly unerring sagacity with which he applies the substance of the method, without its dry, scientific details. Witness his criticism on Sir Walter Scott, and his paper on Boswell, the over-abused biographer of Dr. Johnson, as compared

THE HIGHER RELATIONS OF THE SUBJECT. 181

with Macaulay's on the same subject. And, to conclude this paragraph, a consistent application of the same method would have saved Prof. Crookes and Mr. Alfred R. Wallace from not a little scientific blundering in their investigations of the phenomena associated with spiritualism—eminent though they are in their especial walks.

Assuming that the strictly physiological origin of the very exceptional psychic and dynamic facts enumerated in the preceding sections is fairly made out, their vast importance to scientific psychology is apparent at a glance, not only to the educated observer and the journalist of science, but to the well-informed general reader; for psychology is only an aspect of physiology, as physiology is only an aspect of biology—the life-science, to unravel the problems of which all true investigation tends. Valuable as have been Herbert Spencer's contributions in this field—and it would be difficult to over-estimate them —they must assimilate the discoveries of Prof. Ferrier, and the facts of medical observation now extant, in order to completeness as a system. For example, in the fact that in the cortex of the brain is situated a cognitive tract, while around it is arranged a congeries of motor and sensory centres, specially coördinating the expression of intelligence, and specially appropriated to sensation, the enlightened student will suspect that the nerve-centre concerned in the long-disputed self-consciousness of the older psychologists has been at last discovered. If so, that against which John Stuart Mill argued all his life has an appropriate basis in cerebral anatomy, and Coleridge was nearer right than his acute and subtile critic; and, if so, the guess of Prof. Bain, to the effect that nervous tissue may be thinking tissue, is verified. And this fact dips so deep into the issues of biological speculation, that Herbert Spencer must modify his definition of life to read somewhat as follows: *Life is self-activity, through continuous adjustment of internal relations to external relations.*

Here, then, finally, have the often-scouted experimentalists of the nineteenth century furnished the physiological basis for a system of psychology that shall be rigidly inductive, and yet shall afford ample verge for the softer spiritual undertones of the instrument called man, and for his mystic cognition of the ultimate reality, without forcing him for consolation to the spectral *séances* of Mr. Home.

THE END.

www.ingramcontent.com/pod-product-compliance
Lightning Source LLC
Chambersburg PA
CBHW032149160426
43197CB00008B/839